Predictable
Corporate
Sales

Predictable Corporate Sales

Demystify, Take Control, and Consistently Win Corporate Sales without Cold-Calling, Referrals, or Losing Your Mind

Duane Glader, MBA

38 Years from the School of Hard Knocks, corporate sales and sales management

ARCHWAY PUBLISHING

Archway Publishing books may be ordered through booksellers or by contacting:

Archway Publishing
1663 Liberty Drive
Bloomington, IN 47403
www.archwaypublishing.com
1 (888) 242-5904

Because of the dynamic nature of the Internet, any web addresses or links contained in this book may have changed since publication and may no longer be valid. The views expressed in this work are solely those of the author and do not necessarily reflect the views of the publisher, and the publisher hereby disclaims any responsibility for them.

Any people depicted in stock imagery provided by Thinkstock are models, and such images are being used for illustrative purposes only. Certain stock imagery © Thinkstock.

Illustrations by MORRIS business cartoons.
www.businesscartoonshop.com

ISBN: 978-1-4808-1982-5 (sc)
ISBN: 978-1-4808-1983-2 (e)

Library of Congress Control Number: 2015909882

Print information available on the last page.

Archway Publishing rev. date: 7/17/2015

Dedication

Colette, Missy, Morgan, Adam, Justin, Dale, Bob, Jen and Mom.

Acknowledgements

This book is result of many influential people in my career, including family friends, colleagues and customers. I have shamelessly and proudly borrowed, copied and aspired to be like them.

My brother, Dale Glader, smart and ever willing to kick around cool ideas and solve problems.
Dave Gahn, the best boss I ever had and pleasure to work with.
Steve Ganster, a genius in his field and always a believer in me.
Kent Kedl, a playful mind with a huge heart.
Dave Gilbert, Bob Bolt and Dan McNerney, rare friends measured in decades.
Hoon Bee Kuan, my patient Singaporean mentor.
Ed Coyle and Garrin Kapecki, two of the finest men I have worked with.
George Pearce, my steady, sensible advisor and longtime friend.
George and Martha Birmingham, always there
Nikunj Jhaveri, my entrepreneurial brother
Chris Dwyer, for hiring me twice
Jim Kubik, an inspiration of faith and optimism.

Contents

Predictable Corporate Sales Glossary

Corporate: Big Business, Fortune 1000 or any company that acts like a Big Business, usually more than 2,500 employees

Executive Prospect: The executive at Corporate that the salesperson is targeting or engaged with.

Corporate Salesperson: A salesperson or anyone with the goal of winning a decision/approval from Corporate.

Prospect Company: The company that the Corporate salesperson is targeted to win a decision.

Tactic: A method used or a course of action followed in order to achieve an immediate or short-term goal

Attribute: A quality or feature regarded as inherently part of someone.

Skill: An ability that is developed through training and experience.

Sales Process: The step-by-step path that leads to a decision in a sales attempt.

Insight: An articulation of an intuition and true nature of something gained through various sources of learning.

Approval or Sale: Only when the agreement is fully signed or the Purchase Order is issued.

Introduction

John, a twenty something, smart, well dressed, newly earned MBA under his belt, is ready to tackle the challenge of selling to big corporate. The opportunity is exciting, huge rewards are his for the taking and his confidence is palatable. John throws himself into the company product and sales training, soaking up everything he can. The company has assured him that they understand that selling to big companies takes time and they are prepared to gut it out and support him. Finally John is assigned his prospect territory and is turned loose to set the world on fire, blow his quota out of the water and achieve Rookie of the Year.

Fast forward three months....

No one is returning his calls, the few meetings he had were with the wrong people, it turns out he really does not know enough about the product he is selling, his manager is asking irritating questions about what he is doing and the quota seems like a ridiculously unfair goal. Meanwhile there are other salespeople that seem to be achieving sales with ease. What is going on? Needless to say, John's enthusiasm is gone, his confidence is shaken and he needs to make some changes or else face utter failure.

John's situation is not just typical it is nearly predictable. The time it takes for a salesperson to arrive at this point and the exact variables and events may vary, but this situation happens or some variation of the same theme, to nearly every salesperson that engages in the incredibly difficult arena of selling to Corporate.

After 35 years of selling to Corporate and being sold to by Corporate salespersons, I have written <u>Predictable Corporate Sales</u> to demystify and provide battle tested insight that cuts through the bull. My goal is to equip the salesperson with confidence and the tools needed to get the job done.

One of the problems with sales training is that the methodology and techniques tend to be generic to B to B selling and not applicable to the peculiar dynamics and behavior of selling to large companies. B2B can be a print shop selling to a local flower shop. This is a completely different context compared to a print company selling to Fortune 1000 company. Even worse, completely different than selling to Corporate, some sales training borrow from consumer sales methodology based in emotion and a lot of psychology. Hence I wrote this book addressing the unique highly competitive, high stakes arena of winning sales from Corporate.

"Look, let me get back to you while I find out
how important you are."

Note that when I refer to Corporate, in general this means a Fortune 1000 company. Although I have found once a company is larger than 2,500 employees they tend to behave pretty much like all large companies.

If you are like me, you do not need another sales book that preaches about the obvious basics of positive attitude, persistence and relationship building. We all know how important these factors are so I will not bore you with their obvious importance. Predictable Corporate Sales will drill down and provide the fundamentals and tools that build a foundation for a long term, consistent success selling to Corporate.

"I like the look of this new sales manager."

Chapter 1

Yes, Maybe No: Exasperating Corporate Decision-making

"What do you mean, 'maybe'? You're supposed
to be a yesman, Harris."

Not Sold Until Signed

Understanding Corporate decision-making is at the heart of understanding how to successfully sell Corporate. First and most important, you must understand that when Corporate actually decides to buy, it is not official until either an agreement has been signed or a

PO (Purchase Order) is issued by Corporate. In other words, and I know these are harsh words for salespeople; there is *no such thing as a verbal corporate agreement or commitment.* Verbal confirmations, handshakes, emails, phone calls, promises are not a closed sale. At best I call these responses "go forwards" on the way to a potential signed deal. Executives of a corporation represent the corporation, but in the end a commitment decision is only recognized by a signed agreement by an authorized representative of the company.

So the starting point for the salesperson is clarifying what kind of decision they are seeking from the targeted company. There are generally six kinds of decisions that a salesperson proposes to Corporate.

1. Buy: A "buy" transaction is by far the most common and what most prospects assume when they are contacted by a salesperson. The "buy" decision may range from a simple single transaction to a complex decision to purchase another company.

2. Sell: A "sell" transaction may range from the prospect company decision to sell a piece of equipment to selling an operation.

3. Endorse/Sponsor: This type of transaction involves a decision by the company to endorse or sponsor to the public their alignment, approval and relationship to another company or brand.

4. Partner: Partnerships can take many forms, from complex financial arrangements between companies to joint marketing agreements.

5. Donate: Companies are approached regularly to make decisions requesting a donation for a cause or charitable organization.

6. Any combination of the above

All six types of decisions have different considerations and potential decision paths; however in the end there are **only three possible responses** an executive prospect can make to a salespersons' proposal:

1. **Yes**, which really only means" yes" if it is signed. In corporate speak it actually means the executive prospect is interested enough to engage or sponsor the start of an evaluation, approval and consensus process. This is what I define more accurately as a "Go Forward".

2. **Maybe,** which means an executive prospect has some level of interest and it may mean the same thing as getting a "Yes". By far this is the most common response from an executive prospect delivers to a Corporate salesperson. The tricky part is that "Maybe" encompasses a wide array of meanings; including "maybe, we are very interested" to a disguised or polite "NO".

3. **No means No.** It is truly rare when a Corporate salesperson receives a direct, unequivocal response of "NO". Even if the decision is "No" it is usually said politely in corporate speak like, "we are not interested at this time." Even more exasperating, is that even when they say "No" it may actually mean "maybe". Often a "No" is accompanied with a reason, but most times that reason is probably not the

real reason. However the most common "No" is simply a result of an extended and painful period of no response at all. Consequently the Corporate salesperson concludes by default the answer is "No". In other words, "No" may not have been actually expressed by the executive prospect but the salesperson has decided to give up and rationalized that the executive prospect meant "no".

In conclusion, don't take Corporate's responses literally, dig underneath the response and follow the clues.

"Well, I've made a decision on which way to go from here. What bothers me is how it will look in hindsight."

Understanding the Prospect Company's decision/approval process is a critical component of a Corporate salesperson winning a decision. Stated the opposite, a Corporate salesperson that does not understand the prospects buying decision process will almost certainly lose momentum and any sense of control over the outcome. Not to mention the Corporate salesperson's growing frustration and sense of being lost.

A Corporate decision process may include any number of requirements and steps, depending on the nature, dollar size, internal and external approvals required.

The following are 12 common ingredients that may be part of a Corporate's approval process:

1. Issuing a RFP (Request for Proposal)
2. Obtaining a minimum number of quotes from competitors
3. More information
4. Referred to different executives
5. Internal discussions
6. Approved vendor process completed
7. Determine budget and financial rationalization
8. Determine (maybe create) the process for the approval
9. Determine who would make the decision or sign
10. The executive prospect wants to suck information and competitive intelligence from the salesperson.
11. Regulatory or legal considerations
12. Presentation to senior leadership or the Boss

13 Corporate Insights: Decision –making

Insight 1: "Yes" or "Maybe" is essentially an indicator of some level of interest to "go forward" and begin some level of evaluation and decision process.

Insight 2: Do not expect the executive prospect to necessarily know what the process is to make a decision. If an executive prospect does not regularly evaluate or purchase what you are selling they may not have a clue how to get approval internally and will need to find out. I have actually been in the situation when I knew the internal approval process from previous experience and was able to inform the executive prospect "how it works".

Insight 3: Do not delude yourself; a company is making the decision, not an individual. Forget trying to avoid or short circuiting the decision process. Understand it, embrace it and work it.

Insight 4: The sale is not closed and decided until the agreement is signed or the PO issued. This is not throwing grenades where you just have to be close.

Insight 5: The Corporate salesperson's priority and urgency is irrelevant to the buyer unless there is a direct benefit. What bad happens if the company does not buy today? Usually nothing bad.

Insight 6: Companies buy competitively and always consider multiple vendors and sellers, many require three bids.

Insight 7: If a "buy" decisions requires the company to change from status quo, expect a long and difficult process and time cycle.

Insight 8: Corporate time is measured in months (and sometimes years) not days. Six to twelve month decision cycles are routine in Corporate.

Insight 9: Executives do not support buy decisions that are career threatening (code for high risk).

Insight 10: The person that actually signs the agreement is the decision maker; everyone else is a sponsor, either an ally, neutral or the enemy.

Insight 11: For many corporate executives the art of indecision is perceived as maintaining flexibility.

Insight 12: Corporate executives rely heavily on salespeople for market intelligence, trends, competitive information and ideas. A seller has to be able to distinguish between being used and sincere consideration.

Insight 13: Some executives take the politician approach of "deferring the decision" until a decision is no longer required or someone else made the decision.

"'No'! What kind of an answer is that?"

Chapter 2

Lighten Up On The Corporate Executive

Another essential insight for a successful Corporate salesperson is appreciating and empathizing with the executive. Corporate salespeople are far too quick to blame slow progress on the executive. Executives are people just like you and me, thrust in a role with an organization that compels and highly influences their reactions, behaviors and decisions. Think of the organization as one whole person and you are engaging with just one part of the person....the hand, the eyes, the brain, the voice etc. Don't expect that one part of the person will act independently of the whole or least some level of agreement from some of the other parts.

The critical point is that a Corporate salesperson must quickly and accurately assess the level of authority and influence of the executive prospect in order to successfully engage with them and move towards an approval.

"My mistake! You've worked here long enough to know that I never make a mistake."

Executive roles in Corporate can be broken down into five levels.

Level 1, aka the C-Suite: This is slang for the most important executives in the corporation. These executives usually have "Chief" in their title (hence the "C" in C-Suite). The traditional titles are:

- CEO (Chief Executive Officer), which often includes the title, President
- CFO (Chief Financial Officer),
- CIO (Chief Information Officer),
- CHRO (Chief Human Resources Officer)
- COO (Chief Operating Officer)
- CMO (Chief Marketing Officer)

New unconventional titles have emerged over the past years such as:

- Chief Creative Officer
- Chief Innovation Officer
- Chief Customer Officer
- Chief Culture Officer
- Chief Development Officer
- Chief Administrative Officer
- Chief Applications Architect
- Chief Security Officer
- Chief Technical Officer

These emerging new "C" titles are strong indicators of strategic priorities and directions the corporation is striving for. For example, if a company has a "Chief Culture Officer" I would assume that they are seeking change in their culture and view their culture as critical to achieving their goals.

"I think he's going to talk about the company being over-staffed."

Each level increases the responsibility and scope of performance from multiple areas of the organization. This translates to, the higher the manager the higher the financial responsibility, number of direct reports and strategic direction.

Level 2: Senior Manager: Senior managers are high level executives, potentially future C-Suite, that are responsible for the daily supervision and planning that holistically guides the business to meet its objectives. The common titles are Senior Vice President, Senior Director, Senior Manager, General Manager, Managing Director, Senior Group manager

Level 3: Middle Manager: Middle managers are the work horses of the executive world that usually have multiple managers reporting to them. They are responsible to actually get the work done of the company managing the relationships and performance of the employees. The common middle management job titles include title such as Vice President, Director and Manager.

"On the plus side you do have job security."

Level 4: Department Manager: Department Managers typically are responsible for a functional area such as accounting, finance, human resources, marketing, operations etc. Department managers usually have direct reports of the staff in their department. In Level 4, job titles are commonly name the functional area with "manager" attached such as, Human Resource Manager, Marketing Manager, Finance Manager

Level 5: Individual Contributor: These employees are not managers and have no direct reports. Their job is to generate specific results and contribution from their work. (i.e. number of units, $ etc...). Though an Individual Contributor does not have direct reports but they could have tremendous influence and sponsorship, for example a rainmaker or the son of the CEO.

Seven Corporate Insights: Job Titles

Insight 1: Don't assume a Job Title means what it says.

Job titles can be very misleading and only have relevant meaning internally to the organization. Some companies make everyone a vice president, other companies only allow the title "manager". Probing to understand various job titles of a prospect can yield great insight into the decision process, reporting structure and influences to various executives. I have been amazed many times that asking innocent questions about their job title can yield enormous insight.

Insight 2: An executive will only act within the boundaries of their job title.

A classic rookie mistake is to fall for the executive that promises to get something done that is outside of their responsibility. It just does not happen. Corporate is territorial and highly structured to protect the company from inappropriate and unauthorized decisions by executives.

Insight 3: Understanding the job title and their level of authority results in asking good questions.

Salespeople get favorable response when they ask questions that are aligned with the executive prospect's level of responsibility and authority. Stated in the negative, salespeople should not ask questions and requests until they understand what is really behind the job title (responsibility and authority). This avoids putting the executive prospect in a position of avoiding answering truthfully or having to say "no".

Insight 4: Because they can, does not mean they will.

Even though an executive has the authority to make a decision, does not mean that they will exercise that authority without consensus from others affected by the decision. In other words, an individual Corporate decision-maker is somewhat a myth; it really is a consensus.

Insight 5: Proposal must be career enhancing.

A Corporate salesperson will rarely get a favorable decision from Corporate in which the Corporate executive prospect is not fully convinced that the decision is a career enhancing opportunity. Salespeople should ask themselves, "What possible bad will happen to the executive if they sponsor and take responsibility for the decision?"

"Stop saying 'you're the boss' - I *know* I'm the boss!"

Insight 6: Executives will respond as trained and role assigned.

Don't expect various professionals and executives to act different than what they are trained and paid to do. For example, a lawyer is going to respond like a lawyer not a marketing person. An accountant is going to respond like an accountant not a salesperson.

Insight 7: If they were an entrepreneur they would not be working for Corporate.

Corporate executives are not entrepreneurs or they would have their own business. Don't expect the executives to respond with wild enthusiasm to new ideas, in fact no matter how proven or "cool" the new idea, expect a cautious and skeptical reaction.

In summary, one of the fundamental quests of a Corporate salesperson is to determine the span and depth of responsibility of the executives they encounter. In general it is not what it appears on the surface. Probe and dig until you know.

Chapter 3

Corporate Executives are Driven by Time and Fear

I realize describing our beleaguered corporate executives as driven by "Time and Fear" is not a very nice portrayal, but as a savvy Corporate salesperson, it is all about calling it as you see it. Over the years I have consistently experienced validation that these are the two driving factors in their day to day life on the job. Let's breakdown what I mean by these two factors.

Driving Factor: TIME

The TIME factor for executives includes two dimensions

- ➤ **Time Priorities:** Constant pressure of making decisions of how to spend and allocate their time. Balancing company priorities, relationships, family....
- ➤ **Deadlines:** Constant pressure to provide results within expectations of the boss and company.

There have been a lot of studies done on how executives spend their time. In general, about 50% to 60% is in meeting and conference calls, about 20% to 30% goes to travel/commute, personal activities, about 10-15% working alone (reading reports and preparing for presentations) 10-20% on the phone and email.

So a 62 hour week, would look something like this:

30 hours: Meetings and Conference calls
12 hours: Phone and Email
8 hours: Working Alone
12 hours: Personal activities/travel/Commute

It does not take a rocket scientist to see that an executives life is constantly challenged and faced with the "who, what, when, where" of how spend their time. This pressure means the executive must set priorities and say "no" or simply ignore request for their time. Given this time demand, it should go without saying a salesperson must respect and be empathetic of the executive's time.

A Corporate salesperson can show respect for the executive prospects time with some common sense manners. Respect for their time starts by always being on time, getting to the point, and most important offer to end the meeting when promised.

Secondly, the Corporate salesperson needs to be realistic about the time allotment that is available. If you are given 15 minutes, plan a 15 minute agenda as opposed to trying to keep the meeting going as long as possible. I constantly hear Corporate salespeople bragging about how they scheduled a 15 minute that went for 70 minutes. This may or may not be a good thing.

Additionally, utilization of communication alternatives is far more efficient and appreciated than always insisting on a face-to-face meeting. I find that once a relationship is established, phone and email are far more efficient and accessible to the executive.

Another tip is to shrewdly seek out the prospect executive whose responsibility aligns with salesperson's offering versus trying to call to high up (or too low) where the priority is lost in the crowd of issues.

"He's always late - he says he doesn't like to be kept waiting."

Driving Factor: FEAR

"Fear" is not necessarily a bad factor and serves as nature's method of an early warning system. On the other hand, living in a constant state of some level of "fear" will causes various levels of stress, indecisiveness, premature decision-making, lack of objective reasoning and generally can take the fun out of everything. Remember most executive decisions are not penalized for taking a long time to make a decision, but are crushed when they make a quick decision that turns out badly.

So what really are executives afraid of? Here is the list I have gathered over the years:

- ➢ First and foremost, fear of failing and losing their job.
- ➢ Fear of making the wrong decision and being responsible for the consequences.
- ➢ Fear of what other people in the company will think.
- ➢ Fear of not making their "numbers" and missing their bonus.
- ➢ Fear of being over budget.
- ➢ Fear of embarrassing the company or their boss.
- ➢ Fear of changing from the routine and comfortable.
- ➢ Fear of technology changes and learning new technologies.
- ➢ Fear of not pleasing their boss.
- ➢ Fear of someone being mad and mean to them.
- ➢ Fear of competitors.
- ➢ Fear of the wrong data.
- ➢ Fear of not making a decision.
- ➢ Fear of making a decision
- ➢ Fear of saying "NO"
- ➢ Fear of Saying "YES"

Corporate executives play a role in a grand production. Corporate executives have multiple, overt and subtle sources of fear and decision prioritizing their time and energy. Corporate salespeople must not to judge the merits of these fears, but rather learn to identify and understand the nature of the driving fears, in order that the salesperson then recognizes an opportunity for your offering to address their fears and how to empathically communicate a solution.

Chapter 4

Like Family, Corporate is Dysfunctional

"I'm looking for somebody who thinks big on a small salary."

A friend of mine is a marriage and family counselor. We were discussing the similarities between family relationship systems and corporate relationship systems. He made a very interesting point;

every family has some degree of dysfunctionality. Whether the dysfuctionality is harmful, is dependent on how clearly the dysfunctional pattern is recognized, addressed and managed by its members. He further commented on the interesting pattern that many people are able to astutely identify dysfunctional patterns in other families but unable (or unwilling) to identify the dysfunctionality in their own family. Even more enlightening, this inability to assess their own family persists even if the dysfunctionality is exactly the same as their own family's dysfunctionality.

Applying my counselor friends' therapeutic model to the Corporate, all companies are dysfunctional to some degree. The question is how well the leaders and employees recognize, address and manage their particular dysfunctionality? As salespeople to Corporate, analyzing and recognizing how clearly and honestly organizations work and do not work is not only a required skill it is practically an Olympic level sport.

Just as people have a hard time being objective about their own family's foibles, salespeople typically do the same thing with their own company. More often than not the salesperson develops a combative, negative and judgmental relationship toward their own company. I have found that salespeople that without hyper judgment are willing to objectively and honestly evaluate their own company become much more adept at understanding the prospect's company. I am suggesting that there is an opportunity to increase the salesperson success by taking charge of their relationship and perspective of their own company.

"Just because I agree with you Tom, it doesn't mean you are right."

A salesperson's healthy understanding of their own company is an underutilized tool to increase a salesperson success is developing a healthy perspective and enjoyment of a prospect company. For the most part, I have found it is up to the salesperson to do make mental shift to this principle. Stated in the negative, if a salesperson cannot find a positive perspective and pride in working for their company, life is too short, find another company or conclude you are unwilling to take responsibility for your own perspective and will never be happy.

For a salesperson to develop a healthy perspective on their own company and a prospect company, consider the following perspective realignment provided from some stereotypes I have gather over the years.

"It's not important that we understand each other - just as long as you understand me."

Ten Corporate Somewhat True Stereotypes:

As we know stereotypes may work until you specifically apply them to an individual, so take these with a grain of salt and apply cautiously. I think it is healthy to surgically look at a company and their executives with the goal of understanding versus judging whether it is good or bad. Maybe a better way to think of these stereotypes is theories that need to be tested and evaluated.

1.   **Companies change when they have to, not because they want to, inspired or because it is right or wrong.**

Though there is a great deal of discussions in companies about strategic and operational changes, change usually does not actually get executed until there is a tangible driving force that is threatening the way the company is currently operating. More specifically a threat to the financial performance of the company. Financial threats can be cost increases, new technologies, competitors, regulatory, law suits, the list is endless.

Application Tip: Just because there is discussion about change does not mean that they will change, dig down to the driving sources.

2. Growth (revenue increasing).

The ultimate driving force of business is growth. In our hyper competitive marketplace, if you are not growing you are dying. This explains why a company stock can be valued very low even though the company is very profitable but showing no growth. Growth can be deceptive because there is usually disproportionate growth in various niches of the company's revenue.

Application Tip: Assess the growth pattern and drill down to the segments where the growth is coming from (or not coming from) and you will gain insight to their true motivations.

3. Credit is given for top line results not for saving money:

Companies value contributions to the top line revenue more than profit margin. In other words, a salesperson that brings in a million dollar deal that the company ends up losing $100,000 to deliver is still more highly valued, receives accolades and commissions as opposed to the shrewd executive in finance that figures out a way to save $200,000 of expenses. The business world is full of executives that can cut costs and say "no". It is far rarer to find executives that can actually generate incremental revenue. Companies assume they can find a way to make sales profitable, but there is nothing to make more profitable if there is no new business.

Application Tip: A sale is a sale; bring it in no matter what until someone stops you.

4. The scorecard is money and the P&L has no friends.

In sports, there is a winner based on the most points. In the end it does not matter if the win due to a bad call by the referee, the key player got injured or that it was decided by a tie breaker. The final score has no friends, it is just the fact. In business the score is the financial statement. The financial statement is without a soul and reflects what it is without passion, feelings or friends.

Application Tip: Do not expect companies to ignore the realities of their financial condition.

"We only employ first-class salespeople because we produce inferior products."

5. Companies have trouble telling the truth.

When it comes to getting information out of executives there are…

- ➢ some things can't tell you,
- ➢ some things they can tell you but don't want to
- ➢ some the things they can only tell you part

The point is you will rarely get the whole picture from an executive. There are so many competing stakeholders and self-serving interests in what goes on in a company that getting to the truth can be nearly impossible.

Application Tip: Accept that you will never be able to understand the whole truth and in the part that you don't know may reveal the driving insight and explanation.

6. Executives are basically out of touch with the rank and file.

Top executives of the company are general very smart, objective and responsible people. The problem is they operate in a somewhat isolated world that presents them day after day with a rose colored filter on what the rank and file are really thinking and experiencing. For the most part, over time senior executives become isolated from trusted people in the rank and file that can tell them when they are "full of shit". Evidence of this is the huge industry of management consulting that has been created to try and connect company strategy desired by senior management to actual execution throughout the company.

Application Tip: Find a constructive way to provide feedback to senior management that helps you and them to close the gap; they will appreciate you for doing so.

7. Not a democracy.

We live in a democracy that tends to create a belief in employees that the company should also behave somewhat as a democracy where everyone is heard and has a say in what the company does. Corporate is more like a benevolent dictatorship, whose power is at the pleasure of the owners (stockholders).

Application Tip: If you want a voice in the company, align and deliver results with what the leadership wants to accomplish.

8. Top salespeople rule.

The top salespeople in a company bend the rules, show up late, and receive special treatment, as long as they continue to hit the numbers. Bosses tend to stay out of their way and look the other way, again as long as they deliver the numbers.

Application Tip: Keenly observe and learn from the top salespersons in your company and beat them.

9. What's not being talked about in management is going well.

For the most part management spends the majority of their focus on problems and things that are not working. If they are not discussing a particular issue or employee it is likely not to be a problem and there is general contentment with its status.

Application Tip: Take note of whom and what is the topic and focus of management.

10. When the income goes down, salespeople are always blamed first.

When sales stall or decline, management almost always first assumes that the salesforce is slacking. This is opposed to taking a hard assessment of competition, external forces in the marketplace or problems with the product itself.

Application Tip: If sales are down because of reasons other than salesforce execution, be patient, the company will get there eventually after they are done beating up the salesforce.

"Well, that didn't take long."

Chapter 5

Critical Attributes and Skills of a Corporate Salesperson

Over the years I have worked with and observed many successful Corporate salespeople and a clear set of attributes are common to all of them. No one possesses all of these attributes equally. Some of these attributes come naturally; some are honed and developed through training and coaching. Most likely the largest contributor and refiner is real life field experience. All talented salespeople find a way to lean on their natural strengths and shore up their weaknesses.

When I discuss a successful Corporate salesperson, I am referring to a consistent producer over an extended period of time. Anyone can hit the ball like Tiger Woods one time, what is impressive is to hit the ball so well time after time, year after year. I can't count the number of one hit wonders and Rookie of the Year salesperson that were never heard from again. Perhaps even worse, is the Corporate salesperson that simply never had any meaningful success and are simply "let go" at great cost to the company and frustration of the salesperson.

I have identified a set of ten success attributes that form the foundation that a long term consistent successful career in sales to Corporate can be built on.

Supreme Attribute: Credibility

10 Supporting Attributes:

1. Passionate
2. Managed Impatience.
3. Empathic
4. Storytelling
5. Articulate vision, manage expectation
6. Self-awareness
7. Keen observers
8. Define their own success
9. Ask in a way that they can say yes
10. Develop Personal and Back Channel Support and Resources

"You know what I like about you, George. You say 'yes' with conviction."

Credibility, the supreme attribute.

There are ten attributes, but really if you sum it all up there is one biggie, CREDIBILITY. Credibility is a summation of all the attributes and is a non-negotiable in the world of Corporate selling. So CREDIBILITY is the starring lead role and the nine other attributes are the important supporting cast that I will cover in the next chapter.

Credibility is the mother of all attributes. Simply stated, Corporate does not buy and sign agreements with companies and salespersons that are not credible. Price, terms, features, testimonials and connections are all secondary and irrelevant if there is not respectable level of credibility.

"People like sincerity - learn to fake that and you've got it made."

What is credibility?

Webster's' dictionary defines it as, "the quality or power of inspiring belief." Close synonyms that come to mind are believable, trustworthy and reliable.

In day to day Corporate interaction and communication the label "credibility" is not usually utilized; instead indicators of credibility are expressed indirectly and informally such as:

- ➤ "She is good people, very smart."
- ➤ "He is very helpful."
- ➤ "Yea, I like him."
- ➤ "She is not a typical salesperson."
- ➤ "He is very impressive."
- ➤ "It's an interesting company (or product)."
- ➤ "I think we should meet again."
- ➤ "I think you should join us at our next meeting."

So how does a Salesperson actually get "Credibility"?

Here is the counter intuitive insight: Credibility is yours to lose. Don't shoot yourself.

When the Corporate salesperson first meets the executive prospect, they generally assume or assign credibility to the salesperson, **until** the salesperson provides evidence and behavior that damages and reduces their credibility. The executive prospect generally assumes that you would not have the job unless you were qualified and had a certain level of professional skills and knowledge. Make no mistake, credibility erosion or meltdown can happen in a nano second as well.

Again the principle; credibility is for the salesperson to lose. If this principle is embraced by the Corporate salesperson, a radical change can take place with their attitude and persona. They are free from "trying" to impress and earn credibility. They are freed from trying to "act" smart.

Think of this as similar to starting a college course. On the first day the professor assumes that all the students have the capability and opportunity to earn an A. The teacher does not know the students and assumes that there will be the predictable range of grades. However, the teacher does not presume who will get the various grades; the teacher waits to judge what the student actually does or more specifically what the student does not do. So over the span of the course, the students' action and performance actually determines the extent of the erosion from the presumed "A" that they started with. Corporate executives behave very much like the teacher when it comes to assessing credibility.

Some common examples of how a salesperson's' self-inflict their credibility:

> Being ridiculously aggressive about getting the appointment.
> Unprepared and lack of knowledge which generates stupid questions. (Yes, there are stupid questions.)
> Insisting on reciting their resume and credentials to prove how credible they are.
> Not wearing the proper attire, inappropriate behavior, comments and manners.
> Asking questions that can be answered by reading their web site or a Google search.
> Closing or asking for a commitment before the prospect is ready or authorized.

- ➢ Unacceptable "say-do" gaps. If you say it ---do it.
- ➢ Inability to identify and address relevant prospect problems.
- ➢ Mistaking a "sponsor" as a decision-maker.
- ➢ Ignoring or trying to avoid the prospects buying process.

Credibility Assessment: How credible are you?

5 = always, 3 =sometime, 1 = never

If I get the first meeting I almost always get another meeting.	1 2 3 4 5
I am impeccable polite and well-mannered on appointments.	1 2 3 4 5
I am always well attired and groomed for appointments.	1 2 3 4 5
My natural personality and appearance oozes with credibility.	1 2 3 4 5
I am always thoroughly prepared for sales calls.	1 2 3 4 5
I am smart and savvy on the problems my offering solves	1 2 3 4 5

A score of 24 or better is excellent. 18 to 24 is average. Below 18, major concern.

"I agree you do have drive, ambition and self-confidence, but what we're looking for is ability."

Ten Supporting Attributes

Credibility is the sum total attribute of the other ten attributes. This does not mean that these remaining supporting attributes are not important; rather the supporting attributes are critical ingredients. All the attributes are part of the recipe, but depending on what ingredients are available and exactly what you are trying to bake, the individual ingredients importance will vary.

1. Passionate

A prospect needs to sense and feel the salesperson's passion. Passion is emotion, feeling, energy and conviction about what you sell and the problems you can solve. Passion is deeper and more "gut" feeling than passion's close cousins' enthusiasm and excitement. Salespeople need to find what they are passionately proud of about their company and offerings. Good luck trying to fake it…..prospects can tell manufactured passion like horse senses a first time rider.

"Why must we always communicate? Why can't you just listen to me?"

2. Managed Impatience.

I believe that "patience" is overrated in sales. In fact I have found that successful salespersons are wildly impatient. Granted impatience has to be managed and channeled properly. If properly utilized, impatience creates urgency; it's a sign of a competitor, a motivator and a conqueror fear. So let's call this useful attribute *managed impatience.*

3. Empathic.

Empathy is the ability to identify with and understand somebody else's feelings or difficulties. The most important concept of empathy is to embrace that it's not about you. A sales opportunity is not about your issues, goals, company demands or your feelings. The sales relationship is about empathically and tenaciously identifying with the other person's true feelings, motivations and problems.

4. Storyteller

The best Corporate salespeople I know are also wonderful storytellers. Storytelling may be about customer experiences, personal experiences, story from the media a completely made up story (parable). Storytelling is more than the ability to articulate, it must be relevant and allows the prospect to listen in a non-defensive manner and reinforce an idea without having to address it overtly.

A close skill to storytelling is the salesperson finding powerful words, metaphors and sayings that resonate with the prospect. They need to be simple, relevant and memorable. By the way, storytelling is not joke telling, though good storytelling can have humor. It is the difference between wit and funny.

For example, a general contractor I worked with when asked by the customer if the concrete would crack, would always respond, "I can absolutely guarantee you that the concrete will crack, because it is concrete." At that point he made a memorable point that set the stage for an appropriate understanding and expectation of his guarantee.

When I sold software implementation projects and the discussion turned to project planning I would always say, "Projects end the way they start." This help set the stage for a good project plan, and I often heard clients repeat the same phase to justify why we needed to work on the planning of the project.

5. Articulate Vision, Manage Expectations

A great salesperson is a leader. Good leaders have the ability to put into words the big picture idea and vision, but at the same time communicate the realities of actually doing it. Like a coach of an Olympic athlete that states and reinforces that their athlete can win the gold, but there will be an enormous amount of sacrifice, disappointments along the way, barriers and competition to overcome. One without the other does not work. Vision without appropriate expectation setting will result in disappointment. Expectations without a vision will result in disillusionment and discouragement.

A close cousin to this attribute is the salesperson as a "change agent". It is certainly true that many times the salesperson's offering is the catalyst for a company to change. Like vision, the key to leading "change" is to link the change to realistic expectations of the challenges and difficulties that are likely to be faced. One of my mentors provided a healthy perspective of leading change, he told me...

"Duane, I really appreciate your role as a change agent, but you are not much good to me or the organization if you are a dead change agent because you didn't warn us about the cost and problems associated with your proposed change."

"Duane, it is easy to be 24 hours ahead of your sales prospect, the art of leadership is running just 15 minutes ahead of them."

"I haven't got any friends - only contacts."

6. Self-Aware

A great salesperson has the ability to objectively assess the impression that they make on a person, an accurate understanding of their relationship with the executive prospect and the true level of credibility. They are able to check their emotions and not hear just what they want to hear (known as "happy ear syndrome"). A great salesperson ruthlessly listens and elicits feedback from colleagues, management, prospects, customers, staff and even the waitress at lunch.

7. Keen Observer

This is another way to say a great salesperson can "read a room". The ability of a keen observer is to see behind the overt message. For example, the savvy salesperson knows that when the words spoken by the prospect do not match their body language, what they are saying is probably not what they really mean. I asked a standup comic friend, what makes a good improvisation comic? It seems the obvious answer is that the person is funny. My friend interestingly replied, the number one skill of good improvisation is listening and keen observation. I believe this attribute may trump many of the other attributes if performed at the highest level.

8. Defines Their Own Success

A great salesperson defines what success means for themselves. Another way of saying this is that they have their own definition of what it means to "win". Certainly there are multiple sources of considerations for a salesperson's definition of "winning" such as; quota, profit, team contribution, time invested, relationships, business problems solved, personal fulfillment...

The point is corporate selling is a marathon, not a sprint. The salesperson's company tends to be short term, impatient and never satisfied. Consequently if the salesperson is to succeed long term, they must develop their own internal compass and measurement or they will always be left to the whims of the company and the market. If a salesperson defines their success exclusively based on their company's definition, undoubtedly they will never quite achieve the insatiable appetite of the company over a period of time.

9. Ask in a way that they can say yes

Great Corporate salespeople know when to ask the right questions but also knows how to ask in a way that the prospect can say yes. A simple example is a naïve corporate salesperson that "asks for the order" without finding out the buying process. Is legal review required? Is compliance required? Who has to approve? If the salesperson asked for the order and the proper questions have not been asked, the prospect was forced to say "no" because he couldn't say yes. The savvy salesperson finds out the process and authority that the executive prospect has to work within and asks for the order in the context of those parameters. The savvy salesperson asks, "Is there any reason not to move forward to the next step of getting approval?" This question is avoids asking them to buy right now, putting them in a position of saying "no". Ask questions in a way that allows the executive prospect to answer yes within the realities of their system and authority.

Along with this attribute great salespersons have the ability to know the answer before they ask for the order? Contrary to the consumer model of selling, every "no" is closer to a "yes", Corporate selling requires avoiding an executive prospect from saying "no" and keep the momentum and approval process in play.

10. Develop Personal Back Channel Support and Resources

Great Corporate salespersons have an uncanny way of building an informal system of support and information. The salesperson's companies are always adjusting to the market and there is usually an "understanding gap" between the realities of the field and what management would like. This dynamic requires that a successful salesperson develops informal channels of support and information within their company to get things done, in spite of bureaucracy and cumbersome policies.

"This one shows the time and money spent on making graphs."

Chapter 6

Six Critical Skills of a Successful Corporate Salesperson

Attributes are substantially inherent to a salesperson. A "skill" is an ability that is developed through training and experience. The following are critical "skills" that are common to a successful Corporate salespersons.

The six critical skills are:

- Corporate Salesperson Skill #1: Preparation: Relevant Intelligence, the Invisible Differentiator
- Corporate Salesperson Skill #2: Poise Great questions; Intentional sequential questions
- Corporate Salesperson Skill #3: The devil is in the detail
- Corporate Salesperson Skill #4: Identifying a Problem to Solve: Cheaper, Better, Faster
- Corporate Salesperson Skill #5: The Three "...izes": Summarize, Dollarize and Rationalize
- Corporate Salesperson Skill #6: Negotiating: the end game of the sales process

Corporate Salesperson Skill #1: Preparation: Relevant Intelligence, the Invisible Differentiator

We all agree that "research" before contacting a prospect is a good idea. Typically the salesperson scurries around on Google or Hoovers to determine the obvious; number of employees, the products, locations etc. The result of superficial research is wasting and undermining the Holy Grail opportunity of the direct engagement with the executive prospect. If the salesperson asks simple, predictable generic questions that can be answered by a quick check on the internet and forcing the executive prospect to wearily explain the basics to an uninformed salesperson. The point is that "research" is the activity but the objective is "intelligence" and "insight".

Tip: Proper research is the first place to gain or lose credibility with the executive prospect.

Four Major Benefits from Relevant Intelligence:

1. Provides the ingredients to ask sharp, probing discovery questions
2. Provide the background to connect the dots that allows the salesperson to recognize a problem to solve or opportunity when they hear it, even if veiled in clues.
3. Enhances the salespersons credibility (perception by the prospect) as a knowledgeable, thoughtful player.
4. Enhances the salesperson's confidence.

Well done, compelling research is contrary to most salespersons' natural inclination to fly by the seat of their pants and over confidence in their ability to figure it out once they get the meeting.

There is a huge pay-off for the salesperson that tenaciously follows research trails until they break through the barrier to "intelligence".

Like Texas Holdem', your entire hand can dramatically change if you stay for that seventh card. I have found that one of the biggest mistakes that salespersons make in their research is that they simply quit too early. salespersons tend to quit before finding that nugget of insight that changes the salesperson's insight from average to extraordinary.

One advantage of targeting Corporate is that there is nearly inexhaustible sources and information available, particularly if they are publicly traded. The ubiquitous information available also can become the challenge of too much information available. I believe it takes between four and eight hours of dedicated time to sufficiently exhaust the research channels and breakthrough to "intelligence".

Another common mistake the typical Corporate salesperson makes regarding research is a bias towards what they want to find. Intelligence occurs when the researcher is open minded, focused on understanding the whole company and does not prematurely leap to conclusions. Certainly good researchers develop theories, but understand that it is a theory and must be substantiated.

Finding information is not the problem, particularly for large organizations. The challenge is to sort and sift through too much information for relevant, usable insight for engaging the prospect company. A Corporate salesperson needs to develop their personal research routine and systematic use of sources. There are six logical categories of research to focus.

"Play around with these figures, Harry. I've given you the total I want them to add up to."

Six Categories of Research Focus:

1. Company profile: Revenue, number of employees, locations, products, stock history,
2. External Drivers: Regulatory, Competition
3. Technology, Stock Market, Media, Industry
4. Internal Drivers: Reorganization, Merger/Acquisition, Divestiture, Companywide implementation/integration projects, leadership transitions,
5. Salesperson's Connections: Any connection between the salesperson, salesperson's company, the prospect company or their executives
6. Key Players: Background on key leaders and identification of likely executives to contact or that are likely to emerge in the decision process.

The weighting of these categories and depth of information needs to be customized for each situation depending on the salesperson's experience in the subject industry, relationship and knowledge of the company, characteristics of the product/service that is offered.

Let's be realistic, great intelligence is not always possible or conducted as salespersons know they should. So depending on how experienced, industry/company knowledgeable and business savvy you are, you can still pull off a successful encounter with an executive prospect.

When you were a student and prepared for class by doing the readings and homework, the lecture made sense and you were able to connect the dots, as opposed to grasping the information and content for the first time. You can still pass the course, but you did not get the maximum value and insight.

11 Questions to Complete Research

So how does the salesperson know they are done researching? Boil it down to simply answering the following questions (and I mean simple and concise answers):

1. How does the company generate the majority of its revenue?
2. Is the revenue growing? If yes, how? If No, why?
3. Who are their top two competitors?
4. What are the top two external driving forces today?
5. What are the top two internal driving forces today?
6. How does the company need to change or adapt to prosper?
7. Are there any connections between you/your company and the prospect company?

8. Who are the specific executive decision makers for your product/service?

5 Ways Research Can Become Intelligence

1. When it reveals the interrelationships of various factors and forces.
2. When it identifies the motivation behind a company's actions and strategies.
3. When it is succinct and understandable
4. When it is objective (multiple and third party sources)
5. When it is current (within 8 hours)

Sources of Intelligence:

1. Prospect's Website.

Don't underestimate what can be discovered on the prospect website. You can pick up the culture and tone, how they want the world to view them, what they are not saying may be revealing. Studying the prospect's website also avoids one of the irritating mistakes salespeople make of asking questions that the answer is plainly apparent on their website.

I suggest starting the research with the prospect's website to start the research. I find the most efficient research approach is to answer my questions from the prospects web site then go to third party sources to challenge, refine and determine why the prospect is doing what they are doing.

2. LinkedIn:

LinkedIn is by far largest and most useful social networking website for people in professional occupations. There is a wealth of information, particularly about executives that is conveniently available. Upgrading from the free membership offers a number of additional research options.

Google: Of course this is the largest search engine available. Refine your searches in the prospects industry, competitors, associations, key people, in the news, industry trends. Less used but very powerful Google Sources are Google Scholar, searches academic papers and sources and Google Trends, providing data on search trends on various topics and related resources.

3. Newspapers:

Wall Street Journal, New York Times and metro business news like Crain's Business.

4. Analysts:

Known as financial analyst, securities analyst, research analyst, equity analyst, or investment analyst are professionals in the securities industry that perform financial analysis for external or internal clients. Their analysis can range from very technical to very subjective opinions. The end result of the analysis is a recommendation regarding the buying or selling the stock and /or an opinion what the trend in the stock will be.

5. Blogs/"groups":

There is no end to specific "groups" to join. The range of blog content can be specific to the company or the industry to angry consumer groups and everything in-between.

6. SEC Reports:

Usually available on Corporate's corporate website under Investor Relations. Reports such as 10k, Annual Report, Press Releases.

7. Industry Associations:

Industry associations can be a rich source of information with white papers, trend reports and industry presentations.

8. "Insider" Executives:

A salesperson may have a relationship with someone that has "insider" experience in the prospect's industry or even specifically with the prospect's company. If possible ask the source all the questions in this chapter.

Caution! Even though your source is an "insider" does not mean that their insight or assessment is objective or correct. Test and confirm from other sources if possible the information received. The two common problems with relying too heavily on "insiders" perspectives is that their experience may not be relevant to the specific part of the prospects organization that the salesperson needs to penetrate. Second, unless the "insider" is currently active with the company or industry, their information may be archaic or provide a salesperson with a major miscue. Things are always changing and can change very fast at Corporate.

TIP: Corporate research is extremely perishable.

This means all your great research and insight may miss the mark if you did not freshen the research at least 24 hours before the contact with the prospect. For example, the company was just acquired, announced layoffs; Federal government is on a warpath. Large companies are usually one major event or crisis away from a time and attention, game changing factor. The point is don't get embarrassed by missing the morning news.

TIP: Newbie Vaccine is Research

The single most powerful antidote to being inexperienced or simply young and maintaining credibility is insightful, current and creative intelligence. The experienced person may get the same result with less effort and time spent on intelligence, but so what? The end result is the same. In addition to the value of the intelligence, the "newbie" gains tremendous confidence and poise that resonates in their interaction with the prospect executive.

TIP: Preparation the Secret Weapon

When walking out after a sales call with a colleague and I have been complimented on how revealing and engaging the sales call was. Actually they should have complemented me how shrewdly I researched and prepared for the meeting.

Example: Major Airline Prospect

Industry Drivers (External): Fuel Price, Economy (drives business and tourist travel) Unions, Regulatory

Internal: Recent merger with another major airline

The following is the difference between an uninspired discovery question and an informed discovery questions:

What are your workforce challenges? Vs. What are the primary challenges of managing a workforce that 75% are under a labor contract with six different unions?

How is your company coping with the volatile fuel prices? Vs. What do you think of your competitor that just acquired their own oil refinery as a means to cope with volatile fuel prices?

The Point: Intelligent, informed questions tend to illicit equally relevant responses.

Corporate Salesperson Skill #2: Pose Great Sequential Questions

Ultimately There Are Three Kinds of Questions:

Open Question: Cannot be answered Yes, No or with a number. Good open questions reflect relevant industry/company knowledge. For example, "How is the company responding to the latest regulatory change (be specific) that must be making it more difficult to achieve your goals?" A good open question earns the right by the salesperson to ask relevant "control" questions.

Control Question: Control questions limits the subject matter, create boundaries for the buyers response. For Example, "How do you customers place their orders today?"

Confirm Question: A "confirm question" summarizes the salesperson's understanding of a situation and lets the buyer know that you are listening and understanding their situation/problem. The principle is to stay aligned with the buyer and check to make sure you understand correctly by asking the confirming question. For example, "It sounds like _____ is not just your problem, but it is an industry wide problem, is that right?" Or "What I heard you say is, if you had the ability to _____, you could solve the problem of _____. Did I understand that correctly?"

The key to the effectiveness of the questions is in <u>the sequence of these three types of questions.</u> The effectiveness of the questions depends on the continuous sequence of Open-Control-Confirm. Many salespersons ask good questions but out of sequence. This results in misunderstandings and the buyer feeling like the salesperson is really listening and understands.

Corporate Salesperson Skill #3: The Devil is in the Detail

Salespeople are notorious for sweeping over annoying details that stand in the way of their perception of getting the deal done. The harsh reality, particularly in the arena of Corporate is that the skill of addressing, resolving and clarifying a host of details is critical to getting the signature. In Corporate there is no, "We can deal with that later." Details do not slip by Corporate.

The sequence of steps to deal with issues and details is simply:

1. Identify an issue/detail that must be addressed
2. Acknowledge the subject detail to the other side
3. Agree on how/who/when will resolve it
4. Take note and follow up as agreed

I realize you are reading this and like my kids thinking, "Really?" Although this seems obvious I am surprised at how sloppy Corporate salespersons are on details. The benefits of taking charge of details are:

1. Keeps the salesperson in control
2. Generates credibility and trust
3. Prevents a detail to stall the deal later
4. Addressing details can reveal underlying bigger issues and/ or opportunities.

"Now will everybody please turn to page 5 of the hidden agenda."

    DUANE GLADER, MBA

Corporate Salesperson Skill #4: Identifying a Business Problem to Solve: Cheaper, Better, Faster

If you boil it down, all business decisions can be categorized by "cheaper, better, faster."

> **Cheaper:** A way to execute, deliver, make, produce or design for less money....to make more money.
> **Better:** A way to increase quality, value and perception..... to make more money.
> **Faster:** Anyway to cut cycle time of anything in the business....to make more money.

Obviously the challenge is not a lack of proposals and ways to achieve "cheaper, better, faster", rather the challenge is to navigate the decision that must balance the trade-offs between the three components and yet obtaining profitable business goals and expectations.

The critical skill a successful Corporate salesperson is not only to identify a business problem that can be solved, but a problem that the executive prospect is ready and motivated to solve. In other words, if the executive prospect acknowledges a business problem but does not view themselves as the owner of that problem, the salesperson still does not have an actionable problem to propose a solution.

For example a prospect executive in Finance may express the problem with a marketing campaign that is completely accurate; however, there is no problem for the salesperson to grab onto because the executive fundamentally does not view themselves as the "owner" of the problem. Similar to a therapeutic model, the patient first has to be aware of what the problem is and second and just as important, the patient has to take ownership of the problem before working on an effective solution.

A strong indicator that the salesperson has found an actionable problem is when the executive prospect starts comparing alternatives and justifying costs.

Corporate Salesperson Skill #4: The Three "…izes": Summarize, Dollarize and Rationalize

Not only a salesperson skill, but an all-around great business skill is the ability to synthesize and articulate proposals in the context of what I call the three "izes":

Summarize: Express it in a maximum of one page. Provide the sounds bytes, key points, key problems, in other words, the good, bad and the ugly. Perhaps the most important is identifying what is now known or what assumptions the idea is built on that is not substantiated. A good summary actually inspires and generates good questions, not all the answers.

Dollarize: Hey, this is business, translate the idea, proposal or report to what it means financially. Beyond just communicating what it cost, take it a step further. "This proposal will cost $XXX out of the CapEx budget, and will reduce the cost of goods sold by $xxx per unit, increasing our gross margin by X%, addressing the growing pricing pressure from competitors."

Rationalize: Just because an executive wants to do it and knows it should be done, a process must be executed to "rationalize" that it is a good decision and all the effects of the decision have been fully considered.

There are three steps of Corporate rationalizing a decision:

Step 1: The rationalization is to determine if the proposal is aligned with the strategy and goals of the company. No matter how good the idea, Corporate does not step very far outside of their strategic boundaries. Conversely, if the proposal requires a change in strategy, it is likely to take a long time and less likely to turn out as a win for the salesperson.

Step 2: Identify all the people, department, customers etc. that will be affected by the decision. Once the effected players are identified, define how each will benefit and build consensus or at least confirm the stakeholders are not opposed.

Step 3: The question is asked, "What bad happens if we don't do this now?" In other words, is this the right time? If the answer to this is not compelling, the decision may likely take a long time and/ or die of apathy.

Corporate Salesperson Skill #5:
The end game of the sales process is negotiation

Every negotiation has two basic components; content/subject of the negotiation and the relationship with the other side during and after the negotiation. There are three possible outcomes for both sides: Win-Win, Win-Lose or Lose-Lose. Obviously the preference is for a Win-Win, particularly considering the importance of the subsequent relationship and recurring business potential.

"There's no way we can come to a decision, the meeting has only lasted half an hour."

Asking for an order, a signature or a "yes" is the beginning of a negotiation. Depending on where the salespersons proposal falls in the range of commodity to a "one of a kind", there are some harsh realities regarding negotiating with Corporate:

Fact of Life: Salespersons do better when they make high demands.

Fact of Life: Buyers do better when they make low offers.

Fact of Life: The insulting offer is not insulting.

Fact of life: Start high or start low, just don't start in the middle.

Fact of Life: The first number (or terms) is the most dangerous because it sets the benchmark for all subsequent negotiations. Once that toothpaste is out of the tube there is not putting it back.

Four Skills That Can Turn an Average Negotiator into a Great Dealmaker:

1. Patience: The single most powerful weapon in a negotiation is patience. Lack of patience is usually what destroys the profit margin of a deal. Whoever can wait out the other side usually gets the better deal.

2. Clarity: The negotiator has an edge if they are skilled at expressing themselves succinctly, logically and easy to understand.

3. Mastery of Details: The side that has the deepest, specific mastery of an area will also probably be the better negotiator. Knowledge is in fact power.

4. Costs: The more the negotiator knows what everything about the costs involved, will have an edge in the negotiations. Fully informed cost knowledge goes beyond the initial transaction and includes total life cycle and support costs. In the end most things get "dollarized" which requires knowing what it really costs.

"Harris, when I said 'any questions' I was using only a figure of speech."

12 Battle Tested Negotiating Tactics

1. Don't accept the negative attack. This is a form of intimidation that should not be given into. The critical question is, "If this individual is so mad at us, why are we still talking?" The louder and the more negative the other side gets the calmer and thoughtful you must become.

2. Don't accept their ultimatum (I call Big Dogging). Big Companies love playing this card to test the salesperson and attempt to intimidate a concession and control. I simply take the ultimatum in stride and calmly start asking questions about the assumptions of their ultimatum. For example, the buyer says, "That's all I can afford to pay." My questions may be, "Is that based on the targeted gross margin?

Is that because of competitors' pricing? Unencumbered by the price issue why are you interested in our offer? " The point is to dig for the underlying source of the ultimatum and ignore the ultimatum itself.

3. Don't give them an easy way out....the famous, "No Budget". They say, "I want to do it, but I don't have budget." The facts are budgets are discretionary. Budgets are priorities at a fixed point in time and budgets are on a clock. When a salesperson hears this tactic they should respond by challenging the true state of the budget and find out in fact if there are other issues that are simply being covered over by the "no budget" excuse.

4. Beware of the volume order. Corporate loves dangling the carrot of a volume order for the best pricing and terms. The point is to stick firm on the principle that the discount is only earned when the actual volume order is placed. I have experienced many Corporate deals that start out at a million dollars that evaporate down to a $50,000 initial deal for the same pricing that may or may not have recurring orders.

5. Don't fall for the good cop. Even when it is obvious who is the good guy and bad guy, resist the temptation to move toward the good guy. Focus on the bad guy, because if the bad guy is not turned around you haven't lost anything with the good guy.

6. Don't automatically give the Corporate credit for a thoughtful strategy.... it may not exist. I have learned over and over again to resist the notion that because they are a big

company they have a well thought out strategy. The point is, find out! You may find out they are painting the airplane as they are flying it.

7. What's minor to you may be major to them. Every negotiation consists of major and minor points. What is amazing is how the seemingly most innocent oddball point can be a deal killer. The simple act of questioning the other side's insistence on minor points can reveal a lot about their intentions and save a lot of trouble in the price and other major points negotiation.

8. It isn't always price. It is commonly accepted that price is the major source of battle in a negotiation. When a customer becomes unreasonable about the price in a negotiation it is almost always accompanied by at least one other reason. The key is to find that other reason and focus on it rather than price. Don't be afraid to focus on the profitability for both sides. Even Corporate agrees that everyone should make a profit, even though they like to dictate what that profit is.

9. Be Hypothetical. As a general rule, the more specific the other side gets in their demands, the more hypothetical the salesperson should be. Poise questions and comments prefaced with.....”What if....” Unencumbered by ....” In a perfect world....”

10. Never tell them what you won't do. Eliminate words that stop forward progress and communication like, “NO”, “deal breaker”, Can't, Won't, Impossible, and Never. Always phrase offers and counters in terms of what you can do and in the positive.

"We can...."
"We would consider...."
"I think we could....."

11. Learn to say "Says who?" Treat statements and assumptions with skepticism. The more you negotiate with Corporate the more suspicious you will become of everything on the surface and face value. Every time you let the other side go unchallenged quoting price, setting deadlines, dictating procedure or determining the agenda, you are abdicating control and influence in the negotiation.

12. When there is nothing to do, do it brilliantly. If the deal is at a point to wait.....WAIT! With Corporate there are always spikes of engagement and backing off and waiting. Learning how to be a good "waiter" is critical. Back to the #1 tactic and the single most powerful negotiating tool, PATIENCE.

"That's what I want to say. See if you can
find some statistics to prove it."

Chapter 7

What Are You Selling?

One of the fundamental building blocks of a successful sales encounter is the salesperson's clear and objective assessment and understanding of what they are selling. The primary benefit of objective assessment is that it allows the salesperson to recognize the "match" to the customers need when it presents itself. It is like miner digging and panning for gold, but not really sure how to recognize what the gold when they see it.

A salesperson must build a profile of what they are selling and confidently understand how it fits into the marketplace?

"Will you tell him the sales rep who laughs at all his jokes is here."

16 Questions to Answer About What You Are Selling:

1. Is it a product, service, product that includes service, product plus service, an alliance, endorsement or partnership?
2. Is the product purchased in a single transaction, money up front with recurring costs or no direct costs associated?
3. Is the product itself about the same as other offerings, substitution offering or a new offering in the marketplace?
4. What is the "sweet spot" employee size? Under 100, 100-500, 500 to 2500, 2500 or more, Fortune 1000 Fortune 500, Fortune 100, Global 500
5. How does your company size compare to the companies you are selling to?
6. Who are the users (effected) by the product? Enterprise wide, Region, Departments, Department, Individual (Supply Chain)

7. Is the product paid for from a CapEx (Capital Expenditure) budget or an operating budget?
8. What is the title(s) that are the most influential for a buy decision of your offering?
9. What are the "sweet spot" industries for your offering?
10. Is the price position of your product "low cost, market (competitive) or high cost (premium)?
11. Does your offering have reference accounts and testimonials relevant to your marketplace?
12. Does your product likely require the customer to change the way they are currently doing something now? What job roles are specifically being affected?
13. Who is your primary competition? (See Competition Chapter)
14. What are the three most compelling secondary problems your offering solves in the marketplace?
15. What is your level of product knowledge?
16. What are the common misperceptions a prospect has about your product/service? Company? Industry?

In the end the most important driving summary of all of these questions is to clearly identify:

1. Recognition of the prospect's symptoms of a problem.
2. Effectively match your solution to the problem.

Looking at it from the prospects point of view and answering the above questions avoid the following pitfalls that undermine a salespersons success.

"We could try a 'free offer' but it would cost us."

Know Thyself: Avoiding Three Major Pitfalls

1. Avoids becoming the annoying salesperson that tries to convince the executive prospect that their products solves every problem for everybody? Perhaps the most valuable insight for the salesperson is to understand what your product does NOT do or IS.

2. Avoids becoming the annoying salesperson that is not well versed on how their product fits in the marketplace, forcing the prospect to educate the salesperson.

3. Avoids the salesperson losing credibility by presenting wishful thinking, overly bias, unsubstantiated claims. Remember that prospects often look to salespeople to educate them on the marketplace and be that resource. Take advantage of this opportunity by thoroughly prepared and objective.

If the salesperson has a clear and objective assessment of how their product fits into the marketplace, it will increase their credibility, their confidence and most importantly, recognizing the "solution" opportunity when it presents itself. Obviously it is important to glean as much as possible from your company's product training and resources. However, there is no substitute for your own investment in wrestling and answering the above questions, challenging your company's brochure talk and digging out the relevant points.

Now that the salesperson has determined how the offering fits in the marketplace and with a potential buyer, a salesperson needs to take a hard look at the context of their own company.

Eight Questions a Salesperson Needs to Answer About their Own Company:

1. Have you done the same research on your company as the prospect company? Top two competitors?
2. What do you love about your company?
3. How does the company measure sales success?
4. Do you understand the financial model of your offering and the margins? (costs, logistics, delivery, customer service...)
5. How does the company measure your boss's success?
6. Have you developed your internal network of support and feedback?
7. What are the top three strategies your company is current implementing?
8. What are the top three external or internal forces of change to your company?

"Somewhere out there are people who are still gullible and your job is to find them."

DUANE GLADER, MBA

Chapter 8

Sales Process or Parish

"If it gets any worse, I suppose we could try to improve the product."

We all agree that a good salesperson must be persistent, have a great attitude and good at relationships. The problem is that those qualities are hard to measure, which also means it is hard to do consistently. Over the years I have learned as both a sales manager and a salesperson the key to consistence sales performance and avoiding the typical salesperson roller coaster is the development of specific sales process that works for me, my company and achieves the goals that I have been assigned.

There are many "sales systems", sales process", techniques and advice available in the market. Most companies have developed a proprietary version of a sales process but still the process is usually is too generic and designed for management not the salesperson. Most companies structure their sales process for control, measurement and forecasting purposes. In other words, "helping the salesperson sell better is not the primary objective. The key is to take the framework of your company's sales process and refine it to work for you. A sales process is just another way to say "sales steps". So a "sales process" is simply breaking down the events and path that marks getting a decision from a prospect. The salesperson still needs to comply with the company's procedures and process at the same time the salesperson needs to adapt and modify the process to work for their success.

In order for management to plan their business and anticipate changes, all salespeople, in one way or another, are required to forecast their sales. Sales forecasting is typically a "gut" guess by the salesperson and their manager. As you can guess, sales forecasting is notoriously optimistic and inaccurate. There are really only two sources of accurate forecasting, first and the best, confirmation directly from the prospect (ideally in writing) and second, based on consistent historic time cycles. The value of a well thought out sales process is that the sales steps are broken down and measured in time. This provides accurate data of the time cycle between steps and the cumulative time cycle of the entire process. Obviously by capturing the actual time cycle data, forecast-ability increases, anticipation and expectations are much better managed.

Perhaps the most important outcome of a good sales process is that it creates an efficient system that allows for a much larger volume of prospects to effectively engage. Of course, more prospects means more opportunities. I realize many of are probably thinking that this is an obvious principle of success. However, it never ceases to amaze me that this obvious solution is so often overlooked by the struggling salesperson. Stated more crassly, "the more prospects you have the luckier you get". The point, a salesperson could be doing everything right, but without enough prospects, failure is looming.

"Of course I communicate. You know very well that a grunt means 'yes' and a snarl means 'no'."

A good "sales process" has following attributes:

➤ Each "step" is defined by a specific event that moves the sale forward and can be answered by a Yes/No question.
➤ Time is measured between each step.
➤ Most sales processes have 4-6 major steps to completion

Sales Processes to Corporate Can Be Broken Down to the Following 5 Steps (Process):

1. Intelligence about the Prospect
2. Initiating Contact with the Prospect
3. Response from the Prospect
4. Evaluation by the Prospect
5. Decision by the Prospect

In the remaining chapters I will breakdown each step of the sales process and show Corporate salesperson how to build their own sales process.

10 Benefits of a Good Sales Process

1. Repeatability of a proven outcome
2. Greater control in a process where many variables are not controllable
3. Consistent performance measurement
4. Precise diagnostics of strengths and weaknesses
5. Identify what's working? What's not working?
6. What needs to change?
7. Focus and efficiency of execution
8. Creates accountability
9. Positive, constructive way for manager and salesperson to collaborate
10. Predictability: ability to forecast based on objective and factual historical patterns

Chapter 9

First Contact with the Executive Prospect

Assuming by the time the salesperson initiates contact with the executive prospect the appropriate research and intelligence has been gathered.

First Step: Select an Executive Target

Before contact is initiated with the prospect the salesperson needs to identify and select the executive prospect. This leads to another on-going debate I have with sales colleagues, should you target one or multiple executives? There may be some offerings and organizational structures that lend themselves better to targeting simultaneously multiple targets, but my opinion is that it is less effective in the long run for the following reasons:

> ➤ Multiple recipient messages tend to be more generic and impersonally, particularly if the recipient suspects or finds out the same message was sent to a colleague.
>
> ➤ If one approach does not work with an executive target, the salesperson can adjust it and try another executive target.

Some colleagues argue that multiple simultaneous attempted contact increases the chance of a response based on the simple math of more exposures. My strategy is to eliminate anything that could make my contact with the prospect be perceived as less personal. When a salesperson sends "multiple simultaneous" messages to prospects and the prospects becomes aware of this, they often throw the message on the salesperson spam junk pile.

The salesperson starts by making a list of appropriate job titles and functional department(s) based on the intelligence gained.

For the purposes of this book I am going to define the initial engagement with the prospect executive a face to face meeting. This is by far the most valuable initial engagement and start to building a relationship.

Only Four Ways to Initiate First Contact

- ➤ **First Contact by Referral (Introduction):** a person recommended to someone or for something.
- ➤ **First Contact by Event:** Meeting at an organized gathering of executives.
- ➤ **First Contact by In-Bound Lead:** Inquiry received by the salesperson from a target prospect.
- ➤ **First Contact by Outbound Cold Contact:** An unsolicited attempt by the salesperson to contact an executive prospect that the salesperson has never met.

First Contact by Referral

Depending on the quality of the referral this may be the most desirable way to engage the prospect executive. Obviously, a referral from the "right" person to your target executive provides an automatic level of credibility and acceleration of engagement. However, I have found that "referrals" may not be worth the effort.

Five Key Lessons Learned about Referrals

Referral Lesson #1

Just because the salesperson knows a person that works at the same company as the target executive does not mean they know the person or are in any position to make a referral. Many times at best, a referrer may help you determine or confirm who the "right" executive contact is.

Referral Lesson #2

When the salesperson asks for a referral from someone they are acquainted it tends to stop all the prospecting activity and puts the salesperson in a "wait time" until the referral happens. In effect, depending on "referrals" tend to make salespersons lazy about prospecting. Mentally the salesperson feels like they are doing something by just waiting for the referrer to do their work.

It goes something like this. It takes a week or two to track down your referring contact. The contact agrees to make a referral as soon as possible. Now the salesperson goes into wait mode, the referring contact has a business trip and a hundred other problems and 3, 4, or 8 weeks go by and still no referral. Sound familiar?

Referral Lesson #3

The highest value of a good referral is for identifying the best contact and insider tips on how to connect access. If someone refers a salesperson to a "colleague or buddy", the only relationship obligation to that "buddy" is to maybe take the meeting or phone call. It does not mean that the salesperson has any particular

advantage or obligation in the decision they make. To summarize, the salesperson will likely be treated politely because of the referral, but that's usually about all the referral will get the salesperson.

Referral Lesson #4

For the most part, business executive's ability to refer a high quality introduction for the salesperson's precise need is relatively small. In other words, the chance of the person the salesperson knows has the "right" connection to the "right" person at the prospect company is a very narrow likelihood. At best referrals are a contributor but not enough to build a healthy prospect pipeline as a primary strategy.

Referral Lesson #5

There is a myth in the corporate sales that the highest referral is from the "top down". I have found in reality you may get the meeting easily if the referral comes for the top, but the outcome can go either way; against or for the salesperson. If the target executive feels that she is being "forced" to meet and engage with the salesperson is many times not the best way to start a relationship. . Remember, C-Suite executives are not in the habit of forcing their lieutenants to consider something. It is opposite, the C-suite relies on the lieutenants to find, filter and recommend up to them. Even though the C- Suite executive has the authority; they rarely demand a lieutenant to choose one offering over the other.

In summary, a quality referral may be the quintessential strategy for getting the initial meeting but be careful and realistic what it really is and what the ramification may turn out to be. There seems to be two types of salespersons, those that have mastered the art referrals and networking and those that go cold contact. Success is found by developing both referrals and cold contact.

First Contact by Event (including social media groups)

Event networking such as industry associations and charity events can certainly be an effective approach to getting the first meeting. Again some salespersons are naturally gifted in this environment while others it is a waste of time. Over the years I have learned some lessons about how to utilize events:

> ➢ First and foremost, everyone attending is interested in meeting people for business reasons; however it is very socially inappropriate to show that is your motivation. Additionally, do not mistake attendees' response as necessarily sincere as opposed to polite and diplomatic. I make it a rule that when I meet someone at an event, I will only ask questions about them and never say anything about myself unless they ask. Even then I quickly turn it back to them.
> ➢ Event networking is rarely produces overnight results. Be patient and build these relationships over time and frequency.

> By far the best results for contacts and referrals from event participation is finding ways to be a contributor (not just a taker) and help other people connect. Over time, contributing and helping others will return the highest quality and number of contacts.

"I believe he's a very difficult man to see."

First Contact by In Bound Lead

Similar to referrals, in-bound leads can be the highest quality contact a salesperson receives. However I have also found that similar to referrals, in bound leads tend to make salespeople "lazy" about the engagement and mentally assume that the prospect is far more interested in the salesperson's offering than they really are. I have followed up on many in bound leads and have gotten responses ranging from, unwilling to even take my call or they can't remember making the inquiry. Some actually think I am making it up or they just want information sent to them for some research they are doing.

On the other hand, I have closed business very quickly and easily from inbound leads. The point then is not to assume the prospect is "warm and ready". Take the discipline to treat the prospect like any other cold prospect and the salesperson is likely to maximize the inbound lead.

First Contact by Cold Contact

As you can guess from my somewhat jaundice view of referrals, I prefer to prospect through cold contact. My preference for cold contact is driven from the fact that I have much more control of the process and outcome than being dependent on others for my business through referrals. In general, I have found that "cold contact" can generate a volume of prospects; referrals generate "one offs".

The premise of cold prospecting and contact is that the executive prospect has no direct relationship or awareness of who the salesperson is. The challenge is to breakthrough to the executive target that engages them to the point of responding to the salesperson.

There is some debate regarding the best way to establish the initial contact; phone, email or both? This has changed over the years when the telephone was the dominant approach to cold contact to Corporate. It is true that some salespersons are naturally gifted at telephone prospecting and some offerings lend themselves better to a telephone approach. However, I believe that in general email is far more effective in making the initial contact than the telephone cold call for the following reasons:

- Email provides the prospect executive with the ability to forward the message internally
- Email is far more convenient to the prospect executive to review and respond than telephone.
- Today, virtually no one at Corporate answers their phone so most likely the salesperson will make no contact or leaves a voice mail.
- Email provides the salesperson with:
  - Ability to control the message (particularly if it is forwarded internally)
  - Ability to consistently follow up and repeat the message (create an email chain)
  - Ability to easily plan, execute and track follow ups

Combination Telephone and Email

Some salespersons use a combination telephone first, which means leaving a voicemail, then a follow up email. This appears to be a good idea, but I have found that it is irritating to the executive target. It is perceived as wasting more of her time because it is repetitive. At a minimum I suggest if the salesperson is going to use both, do not leave a long message with all the content that is in the email. Instead leave a very brief voicemail message like…." Hello Mr. Jones, my name is John Smith with XYZ Company, I just sent you an email that I believe you will find worthwhile. Thank you." The purpose of this voicemail is not to "sell" or "pitch" rather it is to increase the propensity of the email being opened and read.

Building the Email

The goal of the email is not to "sell" the prospect your offering or provide comprehensive information. The criteria of every word that goes into the email must answer the question; will this help or hinder the recipient from responding? A response from the prospect executive to the email will be either by phone or email. The message of the prospect's response and can only be one of the following: (addressed in detail in the next chapter)

1. No Response
2. No, Don't Bother Me Again
3. Refer/Delegate to a Different Person
4. Yes, Let's Meet
5. Interested, Want More Information

TIP: A common mistake is for the salesperson to over sell, (information puke) and wild credibility grasping in the initial message. The ONLY goal of the initial email is to get a response that allows the salesperson the opportunity to engage and progress to the next step. Less is more and relevance to the prospect trumps all.

"Relevance" for an executive prospect is a message that suggests a solution to a business problem they are facing and/or compelling mutual interests. "Compelling mutual interest" is what my superstar sales colleague Joe Adolf calls "points of commonality". Prior to Joe initiating a first contact he relentless finds anything that joins the target with something they share, problems, charity, business problem, industry problem, technology change, personal connections, college they went to, trends in the industry....whatever connects!

Figure Out the Email Address:

Do not be stopped by difficulty in finding out the executive prospect's email address. Some executives and companies make it very difficult to find email addresses, while other have their email addresses right in the corporate website. There are third party sources that may have the email address such as LexisNexis or even their profile in LinkedIn. The indirect way to determine the address is to confirm two patterns:

➤ The IP address (@xyz.com) used by the company in their email. This is typically the corporate web site address but to confirm poke around on the corporate website (try Contact Us or Media Inquiries) to confirm.

➤ The name format in the email address for the employee. Usually the corporate website will have somebody's email address somewhere on the site. Companies more or less use the same name pattern for all employees. For example, lastname.first name @, first name intial.last name@. At this point guess close enough to try. If the email bounces back try variations until it goes through. I rarely have to try more than three different variations

➤ Politely inform ("warn") the recipient in the last line of your message that we you will continue to follow up. The impression is that you will keep asking until they respond.

"I'm looking for somebody who thinks big on a small salary."

Nine Questions to Test the Quality and Effectiveness of Your Initial Contact Email:

1. Why would this subject line motivate opening the email? Is it irresistible to open? The only purpose of the "subject line" is to motivate the recipient to open the email.
2. Will the email make sense if it was forwarded by the recipient to other executives internally?
   Every word in the message matters. It is extremely hard to recover from an incorrect first impression or message
3. Does the email communicate with credibility?
4. Does the email clearly explain what is being offered? Is the message well written, brief and precisely explains; who you are, what you want, why they would want to respond?
5. Is the order of the content from most important to least?
6. Is your request (call to action) clear?
7. Is the feeling human and not overly "corporate speak"?
8. Is the gentle "warning" that you will be following up clear? The impression is that you will keep politely keep asking until they respond.
9. Have you had a colleague/manager review and challenged?

Now That the Email Has Sent There Are Our Guidelines to Help the Salesperson Through This Delicate Stage:

1. No response does not automatically mean that the executive prospect has not read your email and/or not interested. I have found it takes between 3-6 follow ups before they actually respond.
2. When you get a response, respond immediately with the goal to set the appointment, not sell or provide information.

If they make any requests or have specific questions, acknowledge and confirm that it will be addressed at the meeting.

3. <u>Set up a schedule</u> of "follow ups" and systematically execute the plan and don't worry about it until you get a response or your system tells you it is time to follow up again. Work the plan.

4. Once the meeting is set, <u>stop further communication</u> and move to preparing for the meeting.

TIP: A common mistake in the sales process that undermines success is the failure to set up a follow up on the calendar and consistently execute the plan. This is a form of "direct marketing" in which one of the key components of success has been proven to be frequency of contact. Too many salespeople will quit or lag in their follow up and conclude that it "didn't work." But in fact it was working perfectly, it was simply one "follow up" away generating the response from the executive prospect.

Chapter 10

They Responded: OMG what do I do now?

It worked and the prospect executive responded. The response from the executive prospect generated from the cold contact email will be either by phone or email. First of all, the salesperson needs to high five the initial win, A RESPONSE. The "response" was the goal of the email (remember "sales process", move step by step).

5 Possible Responses to Email

Possible Response #1: No Response
Possible Response #2:"No and don't bother me again"
Possible Response #3: Refer/ delegate to another executive
Possible Response #4: "Yes, let's meet."
Possible Response #5: Interested, send more information.

Possible Response #1: No Response

Each salesperson and company needs to define when a prospect is formally defined as non-responsive. A have found that it is generally requires 4-6 attempts over 3 to 6 months (this holds true even if the salesperson has a referral.) The trick is for the salesperson not leap to the conclusion that a lack of response is necessarily a lack of interest. Work the process and keep the faith.

Salesperson's Options to "No Response":

- ➤ Decide if the executive target and/or the prospect company are "dead" (no potential for engagement)
- ➤ Final Try. One last communication that honestly communicates your last attempt.
- ➤ Keep Trying.
- ➤ Back Up and Take Another Run at another executive target.

Possible Response #2:"No and don't bother me again"

Salesperson's Response possibilities:

- ➤ Take one polite attempt at getting a reason, " I understand you are not interested and I will not bother you anymore (acknowledge their direction and confirm you will comply)
- ➤ Then ask, "It would be really helpful to understand the main reason you are not interested?" The salesperson will either learn something new or re-confirm that the prospect wants you to get lost.

Possible Response #3: Refer/ delegate to another executive

This message usually comes in an email delegating you to another person in the prospect's organization.

DUANE GLADER, MBA

Salesperson's Response Possibilities:

➤ First determine if it is a referral (introduction) or a delegation (superior to subordinate directions). Referrals or internal introductions are typically for the following purpose:
  - Build consensus
  - Align with executive authority and responsibility
  - Delegation is different from a referral in that there is authority behind the hand off. There is an implied interest and sponsorship when a decision is delegated.

TIP: Salespeople often make the mistake of misinterpreting a "delegation" as approval. Actually the superior is usually just expecting the subordinate to review and come back with their recommendation.

TIP: Referrals are usually a very good sign of prospect interest however don't mistake the referral as approval by the referring executive.

Also, do not assume that the executive that the superior delegates a salesperson to is thrilled with the directive. In fact, they may systematically sabotage the proposal for any number political and personal reasons, nothing to do with what the salesperson is offering. Lack of support is most likely to happen when the proposal being considered by the subordinate requires change or threat of how they do their job.

Possible Response #4: "Yes, let's meet."

Salesperson's Response Possibilities:

- ➢ Get a Time and confirmation of the meeting and end the conversation
- ➢ Do not start "selling". The goal was to get the meeting, don't be tempted to start selling which may move the prospect to a premature negative decision or impression.

Possible Response #5: Interested, send more information.

Salesperson's Response Possibilities:

- ➢ Bargain for a next step. Don't send anything without getting something in return.

The first preference for the salesperson is to not send any information before the first meeting. Undoubtedly the prospect can browse the internet for much of the preliminary information. The problem when an executive prospect asks for the salesperson to send information is that it is often difficult to determine whether it is a sign of legitimately interest or just a polite way to getting rid of a salesperson.

The best way I have found to qualify the prospect's "information request" is to bargain for a next step. The underlying psychology, if the prospect has real sincere interest they are willing to cooperate by giving the salesperson something for sending information. It works something like this:

Prospect: *Could you please just send me some information?*

Salesperson: *Sure, can you tell me more precisely what you are looking for in order that I send you the most relevant information?* (Bargain: I *will give you information is you tell me more about what the prospect is looking for (problem to solve).*

OR

Salesperson: *Sure, can we schedule a time for a follow up call to address any of your questions?* If the prospect will not agree to this are they really sincere?

TIP: Just sending information rarely gets the first meeting with an executive prospect, however, it makes the salesperson and their company feels good that they have some "sales activity". Marketing collateral is for marketing not for closing deals.

Chapter 11

The First Meeting

Nothing Happens Until the Salesperson Shows Up

Congratulation you have achieved the prize of the hunt, a confirmed first meeting. In this chapter I will breakdown how to prepare for and manage the first meeting. I cannot overemphasize importance of a successful first meeting. A "bad" first meeting is extremely difficult to overcome and successfully reengage and recast. First impressions last a long time.

3 Objectives for the First Meeting

➢ Win a "Go Forward" (next step)
➢ Secure answers to your "pre-determined" critical questions. Don't be greedy and try to milk information out of the executive prospect as long as possible. Believe me, "discovery" is infinite with an executive prospect, consequently the salesperson has to take responsibility for defining what is a reasonable amount of insight and information needed. Stated in the negative, the salesperson must define

what is critical "gotta have" information or insight at the first meeting. Without this kind of deliberateness by the salesperson, the meeting typically ends with half answers and ambiguity.

➢ Establish credibility (covered earlier), don't erode your own credibility assumed by the prospect.

Preparing for the First Meeting

To a large degree the success in achieving the three major objectives in the first meeting is directly related to how well prepare the salesperson is for the meeting. Stated realistically, (not a guarantee), but well done, thoughtful meeting preparation increases the odds of achieving your objectives.

You should already have a good foundation of intelligence to work from so preparation should not be difficult. The following are the components of a good meeting preparation:

When and Where: Make sure there is absolutely no ambiguity about the meeting time and place.

How Long: Be clear on the time allotted to the meeting.

Who: Go for a deep dive and find out everything you can about the people that will be in the meeting. Determine if you should bring someone else to the meeting? Who? Why?

What: Define the minimum outcomes of the meeting? Define a "homerun" outcome?

Prepare: Prepare specific information or response to a request that the prospect made prior to the meeting.

Private "cheat sheet" Notes: Create a One Page Reminders for the Meeting that addresses:

- Attendees Name, title, key words about their background
- Top three industries drivers
- Top happenings (merger, new product, new acquisition etc…) in a Prospect's company: Stated in the form of killer open-ended questions. For example, "How is the acquisition I just read about going to affect your job?"

Prepare Your Closing Question: Mine is usually, "Can you think of any reason why we shouldn't move forward?"

Tip: I always prepare a "cheap sheet" to remind myself of the key information, however I rarely need it, but I love having it there if I need it.

Focus and Confidence

Much of the underlying value of prepping for a meeting is that it creates focus and confidence in the salesperson. As described in the elements above there are some very tangible questions and planning to considered and addressed. There are also less tangible, but valuable techniques and activities that if they increase your focus and confidence … …GO FOR IT!

- Stick to your lucky routine and attire.
- Practice drive to the meeting location to see how long it takes, what it looks like and gaining general familiarity.

> ➤ Role play with a colleague and/or your manager. This is probably the single most underutilized powerful meeting preparation technique. It is free, readily available and all upside for your utilization.
> ➤ Confirm the points in your meeting preparation with colleagues, industry contacts, associations and your manager.

TIP: Do not call or email to confirm the meeting that is scheduled. I have found that this can easily provide the prospect with the opportunity to cancel or reschedule. I have found it is better to show up at the appointed time and make the prospect responsible for any changes or miscommunication.

The First Meeting

The moment of truth has arrived. You are prepared, focused and confident. It is your meeting to manage, direct and win.

8 First Meeting Coaching Tips

First Meeting Coaching Tip #1: Time
First Meeting Coaching Tip #2: Start the Meeting
First Meeting Coaching Tip #3: More than one person
First Meeting Coaching Tip #4: Meeting Notes
First Meeting Coaching Tip #5: Game Time Change
First Meeting Coaching Tip #6: Walk to the Elevator
First Meeting Coaching Tip #7: Win or Lose
First Meeting Coaching Tip #8: Win or Lose

First Meeting Coaching Tip #1: Time

Obviously be on time, actually 10-15 minutes early. Big company security can take time and you don't want to get flustered about being late.

When the meeting starts confirm the amount of time given for the meeting. Remember my point about the terrible pressure on an executives "time". Salespeople tend to ignore this factor once they get into a meeting and try to extend the meeting as long as possible. I am all for getting as much face time as possible, but here is the trick….make sure the prospect makes the decision to extend past the allotted time. The technique for this is simple, no matter where you are in the meeting, at 5 minutes before the allotted time is over, alert the executive prospect by saying, "There is five minutes left in our scheduled meeting time and I want to respect your busy schedule." Once this question is asked, the salesperson should not say anything until the executive prospect responds. All executives will appreciate your polite gesture, and many times ignore the clock and finish the meeting. If they want to go ahead and end the meeting you have created an urgency window of "five minutes" to wrap things up and most importantly establish the next step (meeting). The salesperson gains points either way.

First Meeting Coaching Tip #2: Start the Meeting

After the introductions the meeting should begin by the salesperson stating a proposed agenda of topics, reconfirm the time available and what the potential outcomes may be. The most important part is what comes next, get confirmation from the prospect for the agenda, possible outcome and if they want to add or modify the agenda. The result is not only points for just being polite, it makes the prospect feel more in control and you have them already considering the possible outcome.

First Meeting Coaching Tip #3: More than one person

Frequently the meetings with executive prospects will have more than one attendee. Sometimes you will know who will attend but many times it will be a surprise at the meeting.

> ➤ First, I have learned that for the most part, the more people at the meeting indicate the prospects higher level of interest in what you offer. Beware that you might also being used for education and training in your particular area of expertise or market.
> ➤ Second, make sure you get the additional person's name, title (usually they give you a business card), and if not obvious ask what are their responsibilities.
> ➤ Third, mentally put the hierarchy of authority of the attendees. Again if it is not obvious, ask how the organization is structured in order that you are sure what the order of authority in the meeting. The same principle of leading any effective meeting, make sure to involve everyone. If someone is not participating, ask them a question or if they have any questions.

First Meeting Coaching Tip #4: Meeting Notes

Every salesperson has to learn a method of documenting what actually was said in a meeting and there are a number of the methods that salespeople use during the meeting. I have learned the following lesson about note taking:

Excessive note taking during the meeting by the salesperson can be both annoying to the executive prospect and create a strange dynamic. My suggestion is that whatever note taking method the salesperson chooses it should be limited to writing key words and keep your eyes on the executive prospect as much as possible.

First Meeting Coaching Tip #5: Game Time Change

The point of being well prepared for the meeting is also to have the confidence and foundation to be able to make a game time change adjustment. A need to change the approach can take many forms:

- ➤ It becomes obvious that the attendees are not interested.
- ➤ It becomes obvious that that the attendees are not the "right" executives for the salesperson's offering.
- ➤ The meeting started late and there is only a fraction of time allotted left.
- ➤ For whatever reason the attitude of the attendees is contentious and negative.
- ➤ You name it, truth is stranger than fiction. I have had first meetings that had fire drills, announcement the same day that their company is sold and a surprise attendee that turned out to be an old friend of mine. Don't be surprised about anything.

If any of these situations emerge, stop the meeting and simply acknowledge the issue and ask for suggestions on how to proceed. If possible, even laugh about it.

"Can't you wait until I have finished before telling me it's a stupid suggestion I'm making."

First Meeting Coaching Tip #6: Close Question

Assuming the meeting has gone better than hoped and salesperson has his killer closing question locked and loaded. The question is, and this is a biggie, when to deliver the close? The answer is when you have a very good guess (if you have decent people skills and are well prepared you will know) that the answer is yes then delivery the close. On the other hand, if the meeting is coming to an end and the salesperson is not sure if the executive prospect is ready for the killer close, the salesperson has to at least close on the issue of whether to continue with the evaluation and approval process. This is what I call getting the "go forward". Worse than getting a "no" to a killer closing question is to not have asked any the question about the next steps and continued engagement.

First Meeting Coaching Tip #7: Walk to the Elevator

Do not miss the opportunity on the "walk to the exit" after the meeting. Typically an executive prospect will politely walk you out after the meeting. This can be a huge opportunity to get feedback and insight. The context of the interaction at that point is more personal, about them or their personal take on the meeting. I ask questions like:

- ➢ How long have you been with the company?
- ➢ I might float a question about some major event regarding the company or the industry.
- ➢ What is the approval process?
- ➢ How do you think our meeting went?
- ➢ In Chicago, the land of terrible commutes, asking the executive where they live and how long their commute is, can open an entire conversation.
- ➢ The point is, find out what works for you.

More often than not, I have ended up having another 5 to 15 minute conversation on the walk out of the meeting that provided as much or more insight and content than the meeting itself.

First Meeting Coaching Tip #8: Win or Lose

At this point in the process hopefully you have received the "go forward" from the executive prospect. If not you will have to determine if there is a way to resurrect the sales opportunity or whether it's time to let the prospect die from natural causes.

If the prospect is deemed DOA (Dead on Arrival), don't overly punish and get down on yourself. Like baseball, not every pitch can be hit even if it is a strike. It comes with the job. On the other hand, if you lost because of something that you did or did not do, learn from it now. The redemption is the lesson learned wins a deal for you in the future. A sale, particularly to Corporate is a marathon not a sprint.

At a minimum if you do not get the "go forward", learn everything that you can from a loss to help improve your process and performance next time. The following are some good "lost sale" questions to ask yourself. (You might as well ask them yourself, because it won't be long until your sales manager is asking you.)

➢ Have I documented and updated your sales pipeline?
➢ Could I have done better in preparing for the meeting? Specific?
➢ What could I have done better during the meeting?
➢ Did I meet with the right person?
➢ Realistic or not, what would have to happen for the prospect to reconsider?

"Go Forward" can be indicated in a variety of ways by the prospect, from "Yes, I'll buy" to "Sounds interesting". The evidence that a Go Forward has been won is very black and white, there is an agreed upon next step(s) towards the prospect making a decision that involves the salesperson. The next step is typical submitting a proposal, scheduling another meeting, following up with information requested, and a site visit or vendor approval. In other words, a "go forward" has not been won if there is nothing for the salesperson to follow up with and the executive prospect in one way or another says "I'll get back to you", translated means don't call us, we'll call you."

Once you have the "go forward" the most important task is to nail down exactly what the next step, exactly what is expected and committed to by the executive prospect and the salesperson. If the next step is another meeting, nail down the specifics, time place, attendees and agenda. If the next step is a proposal, make sure you have the information needed (or arrangement to get the information) as well confirm the schedule. If the opportunity presents itself, find out as much about the overall decision process, however, I have found that at the first meeting it is better to focus on the tangible next step and save the more detailed confirmation of the decision process for subsequent meetings.

TIP: Once you get the "go forward" nail it down and GET OUT OF THERE. The more you talk the more likely new issues, thoughts and barriers may prematurely be raised that can actually sabotage the "go forward".

Chapter 12

Go Forward and a Decision

You have now entered the most difficult step in the Corporate sales process. This step is actually where many corporate decisions come to die and salespersons are left discouraged and confused. This step also cannot be avoided or short circuited. At best it can be accelerated, but Corporate simply require decisions to be driven through a formal approval and consensus process. No matter what the prospect executive may say about short cutting the process or that they can make the decision, does not mean the process will be ignored. Embrace, understand and confirm the executive prospects decision process and <u>do not fight it</u>.

Five Post First Meeting Activities

1. First Meeting Follow Up
2. Follow Up Promises
3. Manage the Ebb and Flow of Discovery, Solutions, Objections and Details.
4. Momentum
5. Negotiating, the Last Step in the sales process

"You got the order, George?"

1. First Meeting Follow Up

Right after the meeting, I mean within a few hours, write up your meeting notes completely while it is fresh in your mind and while you still have the feeling of the meeting in your gut. Convert the meeting notes to an email to the prospect for confirmation within 24 hours of the meeting. Don't add one thing or suggestion to the discussion. This is a powerful technique that will pleasantly surprise the prospect with an utterly accurate summary of what was discussed at the meeting, the good, bad and ugly. The prospect will be impressed and more importantly will likely forward your meeting summary internally to communicate what happened in the meeting, saving the executive time.

2. Follow Up Promises:

Salespersons notoriously say they will "check into" or follow up on something but don't do it at all or they do it in a superficial unimpressive way. Whatever the follow up id for the salesperson, do it before it was promised and for heaven's sake do more than expected. For example, I was at a meeting with a prospect executive and we were discussing vacations and his interest in canoeing the Boundary Waters in Minnesota. I had just returned from a trip there with my sons and said I would send him a couple web links that I found helpful. The next day I sent him the links, but also a budget we used, a map, a phone number and name of our outfitter and of course some killer pictures from our trip. This executive was so appreciative and impressed that our relationship immediately became personal and productive. I know this sounds overly simplistic, but it I have been shocked at how many salespersons simply ignore these golden opportunities.

Another common follow up promise that salespersons like to ignore is for "reference customers". Again this is a huge opportunity to exceed expectations, don't just provide a predictable statement from the reference customer, and offer the executive prospect to have a conference call with an executive at reference company.

3. Manage the Ebb and Flow of Discovery, Solutions, Objections and Details.

The driving principle at this point is to stay aligned with the executive prospect. The salesperson with the most discipline, most responsiveness, shrewd understanding and helpful to the decision process, has the highest probability (not guarantee) of winning. On the other hand, if a salesperson does not execute these disciplines, they will almost surely lose.

4. Momentum

Every salesperson (and manager) knows that when the momentum in a sales process is stalled, there is trouble. Great salespeople have a way have keeping momentum in the sale and jump starting it when it is stalled. Momentum is one of those intangibles that directly reflect what is really going on in a sales process. Some typical momentum indicators are how fast phone calls and emails are returned, the speed and diligence of post meeting assignments are performed, and if the executive prospect has a "say-do" gap.

5. Negotiating, the Last Step in the sales process

During this step of evaluation usually price, terms and other negotiate points will be raised. Negotiating is the process of compromise by parties to find a mutually agreeable arrangement.

Principal vs. Broker

The roles of the salesperson and the executive prospect are representative of their companies. In other words, it isn't driven by their personal benefit, rather the benefit of their company. This is an important distinction because it allows both the salesperson and the prospect executive to play their role as a "broker" as opposed to a "decision-maker" in their respective organizations. A "broker" is an agent role for the company which allows a much more comfortable role of "going back for approval" or "let me see what I can do" or "sounds reasonable to me, I will do my best to convince my company."

Big companies ignore your price and terms.

For the most part, Corporate announce to the vendor what they will pay and the terms of payment. To some degree a Corporate knows they can bully the terms simply because of their size and their past experiences with other vendors. On the other hand, it is important to understand why they want to buy for certain terms and their rationale. You may discover there are some very specific reasons that are perfectly reasonable. A common rationale is simply competitor offerings and budget constraints.

TIP: Don't get rattled by the Corporate's reaction to your proposal. Stay calm, dig underneath the response and find the middle ground. Likewise, be prepared to counter the response with a thoughtful rationale of your own.

20 Ways Corporate Can Stall
(Not Stalling is the exception to the rule)

Stall #1: Non- Disclosure Agreement (NDA)

An NDA may be required, depending on what the offering to the company entails, the policy of the company or particularly if the offering requires the prospect to reveal internal proprietary financial information or intellectual property. Large companies have standard NDA's; however salespeople are rarely authorized to sign them. The NDA must be signed by an authorized executive of the company. This means there is a review process, which may likely mean legal review. If there is a legal review that means that there will be proposed changes (they can't help themselves), which in turn means that the prospect company's legal will have to review the proposed changes. You get the idea, time is bleeding and they have not even gotten the decision regarding the salesperson's offering.

Stall #2: Legal Review:

Again depending on the nature of your offering and the prospects policies, legal review (corporate talk for legal approval) may be required before a decision can be finalized. Much like the NDA process, it can easily chew up tons of time in the process, giving the prospect executives a perfectly logical rationale to spend time on other issues instead of your proposal.

Tip: Corporate executives do not usually send a proposal for legal review unless they have decided to do it. Legal review is just that, not usually a business case review. The legal review primary objective is to limit liability and reasonable control the contractual relationship as much as possible.

Guidelines for Managing NDA and Legal Review

➢ Salesperson to their own legal
  • Provide business background and relevant issues to help them understand he business context of the agreement for review.
  • Get a time commitment for turnaround time and check in to see of it is still on time.
  • Once you receive the modifications from legal, force yourself to think it through and understand every one of the changes. If you can't understand the reason (in layman terms) the prospect will not either. If the modification is not logical or worse a deal killer, don't just forward to the prospect and hope they respond with

a counter. The salesperson, again in the "broker" role must challenge their own company regarding their rationale and objective. On the other hand, don't expect a lawyer to not respond like a lawyer. That is why the company hired them and they are the ones who pick up the mess when something goes wrong.

- I prefer not to let the attorneys from the two companies talk to each other (If possible). It is too easy to lose sight of the business objectives and focus on the details on preference for certain verbiage. In my experience it has been more efficient and more control to maintain the "broker" role between the legal departments.

➢ Salesperson to the Prospect's legal department
- Once proposed modifications are provided, like your own legal, dig down to understand why all the modifications were made. Do not judge at this point, simply understand. Forward your perspective of the proposed modifications when it goes to your legal.

Stall #3: Compliance:

Some companies will require a compliance review to confirm that the offering complies with an external regulatory requirement. This can range from minority makeup of the workforce, to government approval or SEC regulation. Compliance usually requires the submission of information from the company. The most important guideline to minimizing this process is to fully understand the requirements, information requested and delivery expectations. However beware, even if you deliver 98% of the required information, the remaining 2% will still be required and will not be skipped over.

Stall #4: No Compelling Financial Rationale:

The decision does not have any particular financial effect, so accordingly there is not any urgency. In other words, unless the decision is going to either spike income or prevent losing money immediately, urgency is unlikely.

Stall #5: Vendor Approval:

Depending on the policies of the prospect company, the size and nature of the transaction, the salesperson may have to be approved as a vendor before the buyer reaches a decision. Vendor approval may include a financial disclosure, a bond, Non-disclosure agreement and a "vendor "agreement" or any other number of requirements. The point, if the vendor "approval" is required, do not expect anything else to move forward until that step is completed. Also, expect that the vendor approval process is administered by different executives, (usually finance or procurement), than you may have been working with.

Stall #6: Labor Unions:

If the prospect company workforce has labor union employees that are affected by the decision, whether it is in the labor contract or not, expect delays and consensus building if not actual approval. Labor relations are driven by equal parts workforce issues and politics. Companies rarely make decisions that they know will affect the unions without a lot of consideration.

Stall #7: Volatile Stock or Revenue.

If the stock is volatile don't expect companies to be in the mood to be making decisions without much careful and drawn out discussions.

Stall #8: Pending Merger/Acquisition:

Nothing stops decision-making faster than a pending or recent merger acquisition that impacts the whole company. Remember, merger acquisitions often cause a game of musical chairs for executives and decision-making is a cautious delicate game.

Stall #9: Legacy Vendor:

The logic, since it is very difficult to become a vendor to a big company, conversely it is not easy to replace a vendor that is in place. My goal as a vendor (salesperson) is to become woven into the fabric of the buying company, or as I put, to become "institutionalized" in the company. Consequently the vendor is very difficult to replace, unseat, replace or reduce their position a competitor. Do not take it likely if your transaction will replace another vendor. Expect a fight, just like your own company would launch by the threat of losing a customer.

Stall #10: Regulatory:

Just because it is a great idea and the company supports the proposal, does not mean that it can get done in spite of "regulatory". Proposals that are made without full knowledge of the compliance with regulatory will undoubtedly run into delays and problems. I strongly suggest that the salesperson takes the lead and proactively identifies regulatory issues and not rely or wait for the buyer to determine the issues.

Stall #11: Don't have to Change.

If the decision required by the company requires the company to change how they do something, expect a slow decision unless that change is driven by compliance or money. In other words, companies like people change when they have to. Carefully evaluate whether the decision you are seeking requires change or what degree of change. The answer will be highly correlated to the difficulty and time required for the decision.

Stall #12: Travel Schedules.

Nothing sinister about this, but travel schedules can play havoc on decisions process. When executives travel their priorities change and they focus on the purpose of the travel. Travel can also work to the salesperson advantage by pushing to get decisions made before travel schedules delays the decision.

Stall #14: Reorganization.

The dreaded "reorganization" of a company obviously throws decision making into suspense until the dust settles.

Stall # 13: New in Role (or about to change role).

When the executive has been on the job or the role or know they are leaving that role for less than a six months, decisions tend to be deferred until they have a full view and informed on decisions to be made.

Stall #14: Budget:

Save yourself a ton of headaches, find out early if they have budget, when is it available and what are the limits. Just because they do not have "budget" does not mean the deal is dead. There is always money available somewhere in a big company, but how it is approved and secured is a delicate process and usually takes time.

"Can I call you back Harry, I think the restructuring has started."

Stall #15: Wrong Person (Sponsor).

The executive loves the proposal; unfortunately they are the wrong person. There are only two roles for the prospect executive from a salesperson point of view, either a sponsor or a decision maker (signs the agreement). . If the executive prospect is either of these they are the wrong person.

Stall #16: Internal Consensus/Approval:

Corporate executives make decisions by consensus, even if they have the authority to make the decision by themselves. Corporate decision-making includes testing the decision for sound logic and political fallout.

Stall #17: Professional Buyer:

Big companies have processes and departments (Procurement or Purchasing) that are professional buyers. They have access to all pricing and terms available and have absolutely no problem proposing their terms without regard to what the salesperson proposed, discussed or another executive in the company said was acceptable.

Stall # 18: Internal Infrastructure not ready.

Companies tend to make decisions in a linear manner. In other words, they don't tend to buy software until they have the hardware first. They certainly discuss and plan the purchase but the actual decision tends to be "just in time"

Stall #19: Nothing Wrong---It just takes this long.

Hey I understand, we are salespeople and need a decision. What the heck is taking so long? The answer may be that it simply takes a long time and there is absolutely nothing wrong. Relax, it comes with the job.

Stall #20: Seasonality:

Fiscal year, Quarter end, Sales peaks. Most businesses and industries have seasonality. Could be as simple as holiday slowdown or intensity, external factors (regulatory, earnings calls etc…) or product release cycles. The salesperson needs to be very cognizant of the cycles and seasonality and how it could affect the decision making cycle.

Stall: # Infinite" Hence a Corporate salespersons real job…. dealing with stalled sales.

"I'll ask Tom in the graphic's department to improve the sale's figures in Photoshop."

Chapter 13

Managing Your Boss

Your boss, the sales manager, juggles a lot of responsibilities. In a nutshell their life is driven by one major drive; achieving "the numbers" by a certain date.

Anything that does not help the sales manager achieve that goal will likely take a back seat. They do have other drivers that they reluctantly respond to such as;

> ➤ Recruiting/Firing: If it helps make their numbers.
> ➤ Securing resources: If it helps them make their numbers.
> ➤ Forecasting: If it helps them make their numbers.
> ➤ Training Sales Team: If it helps them make their numbers.
> ➤ Advocate sale staff issues will the company: If it helps them make their numbers.

Do you get? It is all about helping your manager make their numbers. Don't fight it, accept it!

The starting point is to find out what are your boss's numbers and deadline, and then figure out how to help accomplish it.

Every request made to sales managers needs to be placed in the context of contributing to the number goal. For example,

"I need an exception to the policy so that I can get the deal done now?"

"I want to go to this seminar because it will help me fill a skills gap I have to close more deals."

"Don't forget to make a note of my raised eyebrows."

As a salesperson and a sales manager I have developed a list of 10 Tips that establishes a successful managed relationship with your sales manager.

10 Tips to Manage Your Boss

Tip 1: You will pay for Happy Ears

Telling the boss what he wants to hear and exaggerating the size and timing of a sale will come with a heavy cost later.

Tip 2: Don't be more blunt and honest than your Boss.

The boss is only interested in the same level of honesty from you that he/she is giving you.

Tip 3: Transparency earns trust.

It is amazing how disarming and how much credit you will receive by simply being transparent and non-defensive.

Tip 4: Beat the boss to the conclusion.

Don't wait for the boss to tell you the obvious in regards to your performance and your sales.

Tip 5: Talk about compensation once a year.

Do yourself and your boss a favor and restrict discussion regarding the comp plan to once a year. Once a year, make your case and make your deal, then put it the fault and stop whining about it.

Tip 6: Never be too proud to ask for help.

The most successful salespeople I know are genius at getting the help they need, no matter what it is. In the world of Corporate no one knows it all. The best source of help is usually your boss.

"I've learnt not to worry."

Tip 7: "Atta boys" last 24 hours.

No matter what your success or deal you sold, don't expect your boss and company's accolades to last not more than 24 hours before they are chirping, "What have you done for me lately?"

Tip 8: When sales are down, sales team is sloughing off.

When sales drop, the boss and company always first blame the salespeople. If the slump is for something other than the sales force efforts, it is only a matter of time before the changes will arrive.

Tip 9: Top Salesperson always gets treated different.

Get over it or become the top salesperson. Every company is the same, the top salesperson rules.

Tip 10: "Unfair" is never accepted as a reason for not making your numbers.

Salespeople are notorious for their articulate expression of why a comp plan, a product, a price, terms etc.... are unfair and if it could be changed the sales would come pouring in. Believe me it is always unfair so get it done anyway. If a salesperson really believes they could make the sale with a change, sell it and ask for an exception with the signed agreement in hand.

"We've just received an order!"

Conclusion

Are you ready to take control and win sales from Corporate?

Here are some concluding thoughts to help you bring the insights of <u>Predictable Corporate Sales</u> together.

Process or Execution:

If you are not having a productive sales success, the problem is either PROCESS or EXECUTION. It is almost always one or the other. Either you don't have a clear and proven process or you have a good process but you are not executing it well. The third possibility when "process" and "execution" are not the problem is almost certainly the market is too small to develop an appropriate pipeline.

Identify Specific Problem Stage:

If "PROCESS" is the problem, identify the specific STAGE that you are weak. Everyone is stronger or weaker in different stages. No one has it all.

Active Pipeline:

There should constant movement in a healthy pipeline of prospects. One of the most obvious predictors of poor sales performance is the length of time and number of accounts at a specific sales stage.

Follow-Up:

The single biggest contributor to Corporate sales failure: Poor Execution of planned, intentional, consistent "Follow Ups"

Happy Ears:

Have you have fallen for the dreaded salesperson malady known as "Happy Ears". This is a condition that the salesperson hears what they hope and is without substantiation. Be ruthlessly honest about where your prospects really are. Perhaps more importantly is to be honest about what you don't know about where they are.

Role Playing:

The most simple and effective form of sales training is role playing. Don't over think it, while speaking to your colleague or boss, just start being the prospect or have the other person be the prospect. Just jump in and start pretending and see what happens.

Credibility, Passion and Confidence:

Don't ever underestimate the importance of the foundation of credibility. Be honest, do you speak and have the presence that communicates and embodies Credibility, Passion and Confidence?

Homework:

Want credibility and confidence? Do your homework better than anyone would ever expect.

Boring and Predictable:

Take risks to engage the executive prospects. Executives will respond favorably to risk taking if you are credible, sincere and empathic.

Transparency and Accountability, in other words, No Manipulating.

On one hand salespeople view a company sales process and reporting as a way for the boss to micro manage and direct every move they make with a prospect. On the other hand, this can be a great tool for the salesperson to communicate clearly, build trust and actually lead the boss.

It is my sincere hope that Predictable Corporate Sales will help you accelerate your success and that you will be able to learn some of the lessons I learned without so much pain and frustration. Selling to Corporate is like riding a rollercoaster, exciting and scary at the same time. Happy Hunting!

Appendix

Duane's School of Corporate Selling
(Not is order of importance)

We are all Dysfunctional.

All companies, people and families are dysfunctional to some degree; most revealing is how aware, open and objective we are about our dysfunctionality.

Don't believe the Org Chart.

No formal org chart is how actual influence is exercised and decisions are made.

Companies only change when they have to.

"Have to" change is almost always driven by the threat to profitability. The point: If what I am selling requires the company to change...Beware!

Concepts resonate----products turn off.

Speak to prospects in conceptual terms, unencumbered by our product. Once the concept has been agree to, the product approval is much easier.

Big companies like big ideas.

However, that does not mean they will actually do them (see point#2).....but they do like talking about it. Along with this, big companies like to do business with other big companies.....they just feel better.

Ingredient, not the cake.

Understand how we fit into their larger strategy as an ingredient. You will turn off a corporate executive quickly with an inappropriate positioning that we are a bigger solution than we really are.

No one likes our brand better ourselves.

Conversely, no one likes their own brand better than the prospect. Relax and accept the brand rhetoric and bias. In the B2B space, branding is usually a personal experience with a real person from that company.

Follow Up.....Tell the Truth

The key to an effective written follow up to a meeting is accurately, without adding embellishment and a salesperson's "happy ears" interpretation. The follow up needs to include the good, the bad and the ugly. Actually you will probably get more "points" for accurately describing the "ugly". If a follow up email is done well it is the single biggest factor to spread your message internally via the "forward" button on email.

Decision-maker is the Signer.

Determine who the decision maker is and who the sponsor is. Salespeople hate this but the decision maker is who actually signs the agreement. Everyone else is a sponsor.

Accountants and Lawyers can't help themselves.

In the end, no matter how inspirational, cool and successful the corporate initiative is the accountants and lawyers will eventually dollarize it, minimize and water it down.

Rhetoric and Reality.

There is always a disconnect and gap between the message and strategy from the C-Suite, corporate website message and the general workforce. The only question is how big is the gap? An entire industry of management consulting has been created to serve this problem.

The C-Suite myth. Calling high is high risk – high reward.

Just because you start at the top does not mean support will roll downhill. Senior management relies of their staff to filter and make recommendations, not the reverse. C –Suite deals is big ideas, big strategy and big problems. If what you are selling is not that... ...get a referral from the C-suite to the right person is a win....be careful.

The higher you engage, the more simple and bold

The higher you call, the bolder, more simple and obvious a business solution must be.

Sponsors are the lifeblood.

Corporate selling is about recruiting and equipping (training) sponsors, building buy-in and coalitions. It resembles more of a lobbyist campaign than it does a consumer purchase decision.

It all starts at the top.

Corporate personality, culture, inclusive vs. exclusive, attitude, how they treat vendors all starts at the top....always.

Corporate decisions take forever, unless they don't want it to take forever, then it can happen immediately. The question is to be objective why what I am selling needs to be done quicker than the rest of the normal slow decisions.

Never forget that you are talking to a real person---but they are playing a role for the organization. Their role has a limitation that does not allow them to do whatever they want. Even if they have the authority, they have informal limitations and consensus building requirements if they are going to survive successfully in their role.

How much is the impact on profit?

Corporate engagement (particularly at in the C-Suite) is directly correlated to the impact of the topic on the revenue line, the profit line or both. Rule of thumb is that unless the topic affects a minimum of 5% to 10% revenue or profit they may only be mildly engaged and interested.

Corporate cannot be sold, THEY BUY -----Help them Buy

They buy when they want to, how they want to and if they are Wal-Mart, for what price they require.

www.ingramcontent.com/pod-product-compliance
Lightning Source LLC
Chambersburg PA
CBHW021942170526
45157CB00003B/889